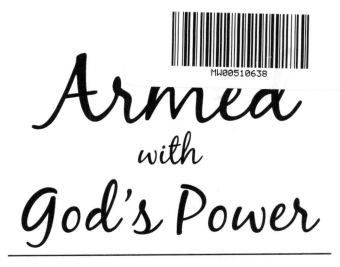

Armed

with

God's Power

Changing Brokenness to Victory through God's Love

Nora White

ISBN 978-1-64468-931-8 (Paperback)
ISBN 978-1-64468-932-5 (Digital)

Covenant Books, Inc.
11661 Hwy 707
Murrells Inlet, SC 29576
www.covenantbooks.com

God's desire is for us to experience an intimacy and closeness with Him where we can hear Him whisper thoughts into our hearts. Nora shares this through her own journey in a way that will lead you to desire to know God better and listen to His still, soft voice. Nora communicates life-changing power out of her life in the midst of personal pain and victory. Her heart's desire is to help mentor women to continue to grow closer to God and help them learn to recognize and respond to God's voice. *Armed with God's Power* has stirred my soul and fed my need to learn to recognize and respond to God's voice—to go beyond the busyness of life and its distractions that seem to drown out God, and really focus in on listening to God. Nora powerfully captures the longing we all need to feel, that deeper intimacy with God.

—Darla Warner
Manufacturing Business Owner
Cofounder of the Side by Side Ministry, Ohio

Powerful, real, down-to-earth! A strong testimony as to how God is at work in our lives even through tough times of struggle. *Armed with God's Power* will shed a new light on how our Lord guides us. It is a great reminder that if we find ourselves in a bad situation, we don't have to stay there. God will help us find our way out into a brighter future!

—Alice J. Fitch
Parent Locate Support Officer for
Cuyahoga County, Cleveland, Ohio

This was a very thought-provoking book that I found both comforting and enlightening. I was able to identify with Nora's story, and have lived with some guilt and confusion for many years due to my life situations. Her story has shown me that my faith can help me recover.

—Amy Appleman
Credit & Collections Manager, AT&T

I have known Nora White for over seven years; this book makes me feel like I really know her. Nora's spirit through all the events she went through seems to be what Peter wrote in 1 Peter 3:3: "The wife's beauty should be that of your inner self, the unfailing beauty of a gentle and quiet spirit; which is of great worth in God's sight."

—Pastor Terry Zerby
Associate Director of Senior Adults
Parma Heights Baptist Church, Ohio

Acknowledgments

To Dennis, Tina, and Geoff, I am so grateful for your tender love and faith that has matured through the rivers and valleys we crossed over the years. I thank God every day for giving me such a wonderful family.

To Janice M. Wagner and Marcia May Kolezynski, thank you for the tremendous job you both put into editing my manuscript. It is not an accident that God placed you both into my life when He did. Your response to His call was marvelous.

To all our friends, we are extremely grateful for the enormous support you gave us over the years. It is truly breathtaking to have such wonderful friends who graciously walked beside us.

Sometimes God sends angels to help us out when we need it. We may not know where they are, but I think I know a few. Thank you.

Preface

*A*s I stand here, gazing around this living room, I can still feel the memories wash over me. To my right is the couch that John, my late husband, bought for me. It was his favorite piece of furniture. Almost straight across from the couch are the love seat and chair I bought later, which match the couch. Over on the far wall is a picture he bought me. It still looks like new, even after all these years. The silver and black etching of a three-dimensional floral print still sparkles in the afternoon sunlight that filters through the front window. There are two lamps that John often teased me about. He always said I did things backward. I guess I did, because the first thing I did after we bought our home was go out and buy those black lamps with the blue flowers, and then I designed the living room around the lamps.

I love this room. Even though John is gone, it still holds his essence. Standing in the doorway and drinking it all in, I can feel him here. Yes, I can really feel him here. If I close my eyes, I can imagine him sitting here, just as he had done so many times in the past. This room holds all the laughter that John and I shared. It also holds all of the heartaches. It was not always easy for us, but we got through. That gives this room a life of its own—a life that has not left here over the years since John died.

Sometimes people feel lonely when a house becomes empty that was once filled with life and energy during special times. I occasionally get a feeling of being alone in a museum of memories. Our room has become a quiet, meditative place. Now I am facing a new beginning—new decisions, a new life—but God has shown me His love, helping me through the happy times, the sad times, and the times of uncertainty. I have come to know that there is no reason for anyone to ever feel alone. God's love reaches far and wide to light the way for us during our times of darkness. We should willingly embrace Him.

I was told that someday I would write a book. This is that book. The colors on the cover reflect the magnificence and power of God, yet you see a kaleidoscope of unique and intricate details, which represents all of us. If only we could understand how special we are to Him. He made us in His own image and gave us the opportunity to come to Him with everything. He is patiently waiting for all of us to reach out to Him.

For years I carried the vision of the cover of the book in my mind, and I gradually came to the realization that I would write my story when the time was right. You see, God gives all of us a vision that is always there in our minds, somewhere. At times the vision may be crowded out by other concerns, but it never really goes away. It remains buried under piles of worldly pressures. However, for many people it takes root and becomes stronger and grows, often bursting through the surface only during our times of trouble and worry. Over time, it may flourish, drawing each of us closer to the reality of the dream—love and salvation.

I hope that by sharing this story with you, I can help you to realize that no matter what life throws at us, God is always there. We only have to be willing to arm ourselves with His comfort and His love.

Chapter 1

$\mathcal{I}$ will never forget how it all began. I was going through one of the biggest crises of my life. Living in West Newton, Pennsylvania, at the time, I had what seemed to most a nearly perfect life. My husband and I had been married for fifteen years and lived in a beautiful ranch home on more than four acres of land. All of the trappings of the good life were mine. We had a two-car garage, spacious rooms with cathedral ceilings, a wooded backyard, and a swimming pool. The best gifts of all, though, were our two lovely children. At the time of this crisis, Tina was eleven years old, and Geoff was eight. No, it didn't happen overnight, but what was once a fairy-tale beginning came crashing down like a train wreck nonetheless. Our lives were so different.

Everything about our upbringing, our beliefs, our backgrounds, and everything was different, and we never meshed. Over the course of time, we began to disagree on everything. Then failures and bad decisions began to rule over our lives. The ability to reason and change our course made it more difficult to communicate with each another. Somewhere along the way, emptiness became the only friend I had. Then the dark clouds rolled in.

My husband lost his job at the mill and he was never home. Our marriage had gone sour. After two years, he found a job in Ligonier, about an hour's drive away. He took the job as a custodian of an apartment complex and along with it came his own apartment. I no longer received any support from him emotionally or financially. Someone else was getting his attention. This left the children and me to handle things alone. After months and months of total confusion and a complete upheaval of the comfortable life I once had, I filed for divorce.

The decision of the divorce and the actual process was the hardest thing I had ever gone through, but we had drifted far apart. The feelings that had been there before were gone. Despite my best efforts, there was no way for me to revive the marriage. It was over, and I was left feeling hurt, lost, and confused.

Up until that point in my life, I had been a lukewarm Christian. I knew the Lord, but I didn't really know how much greater my relationship with Him could be. I called on Him during times of trouble, but I was not a regular churchgoer, and many of His words to me fell on deaf ears. I had been caught up in my life with people and things with which I had surrounded myself. They had seemed to be my salvation and they gave me a reason for being and staying busy. During that part of my life, it was not often that I reached out to God. I was comfortable in my niche, and I thought I had been secure with my husband, my children, my work at Murphy Mart Department Store, my possessions, and my own private dreams. These things wrapped me up and insulated me from my need to seek the love of the Lord.

With my change in marital status came immense pain and stress. My husband moved away from the scene of our dreams and happiness. For the most part, he stayed out of our lives, although he did come to see Tina and Geoff on some occasional weekends. Needless to say, this was all very difficult for me and the children. Everything was in an uproar, more so than I had expected. It was now up to me to handle all of the responsibilities of the household. Eventually there was a little financial support from my husband, but it was not even close to meeting our needs. I felt the tremendous pressure of having to be responsible for everything that the children needed and the many challenges of taking care of the house, yard, car, and everything else. There was nothing for me to hold on to for certain and nothing to pull me out of my growing sense of depression.

Adjusting to a life alone with the kids was hard. There were so many things I had to do—cook, clean, and chauffer Tina and Geoff to school activities, parent-teacher conferences, help with homework, and still find the energy to do paperwork necessary to pay the bills. The tasks were never ending. I hurried through every task, trying to get things done and still keep some sense of sanity.

In the two years before the end of my marriage, I had worked many part-time and full-time jobs. I worked as a jewelry sales representative for Triffari and Monet jewelry, which required me to travel from one department store to another, resetting displays and working with the staff, encouraging them to sell the products. Although Monet and Triffari were separate companies, it was convenient that I could work both lines of jewelry in one trip per store. I also sold jewelry for a home-based business called Act II Jewelry. I booked parties whenever I could get one, even if it meant traveling long distances. I also modeled for Life Stride and Candy's Shoes at trade shows in Monroeville, which was about forty-five minutes from home. I took a job as a manufacturer's representative, selling greeting cards and gifts with the hope of replacing a few of the part-time jobs I still had.

As a manufacturer's representative, my job was to sell various gifts to stores throughout western Pennsylvania. This meant traveling to a lot of places and staying overnight. It was not the kind of job I really wanted, nor was the money as much as I would have liked or needed, but it was better than stringing several full- and part-time jobs together to make ends meet.

My mom, Joan, watched from a distance as I struggled to keep it all together. Just as I was in danger of drowning under all of the work and stress, she graciously offered to move in with us. She left her home in Everson, Pennsylvania, which was about twenty minutes away, and came to help out. She held us together in those days by being a steadying influence on our household and by providing me with some much-needed emotional support. Her presence allowed me more time to work so that we could afford to live.

However, my added work on the job only brought on more stress. Events and normal things that used to make me happy now only filled me with a feeling of numbness and more depression. I once had a life with structure and balance, or so I thought. Now my husband was gone, and suddenly my life was uncertain like a fragile house of cards. Part of the foundation that had been my life was my husband; now he had been removed, and everything seemed to come crashing down around me. Somehow, I could no longer see the color and beauty in my life. The only thing that I could be sure of was that tomorrow would bring more of the same uncertainty. In many ways, I imagined that it would probably be worse.

Those who have gone through a divorce may understand to some degree how I felt. The feelings of powerlessness and loss were overwhelming. It was a daily struggle to keep from being suffocated. Dangerous emotions crept into every corner of my life, making even simple tasks seem almost impossible. Nothing in my life seemed to be satisfying, and my sanity was almost gone. Despite my hard work, the debts were piling up higher and higher. The bill collectors seemed to be hiding around every corner. It seemed like everything I touched, other than Tina and Geoff, turned sour. I was drifting all alone, feeling lost and losing my sense of self more each day.

Tammy, my best friend, was concerned about me. She saw a person who was once happy and outgoing turn sullen and withdrawn. She told me that she was worried about my changed behavior and my state of mental health. Although not knowledgeable about this topic, Tammy guessed that I was soon headed for a mental breakdown. She was probably correct, because my emotions were all mixed up. Sometimes I didn't even know what I was feeling. I would find myself suddenly shaking uncontrollably, rocking back and forth quietly, breaking into hysterical laughter, and then crying for no apparent reason.

It was not as though I lacked help at this time. My mother took care of many aspects of the home and cared for the children. Tammy and her husband, Ron, who were longtime friends, took me under their wing. I was in desperate need of companionship, and they were there for me. They tried to cheer me up and help me think positively. However, I felt crushed by my situation, and nothing they did for me seemed to work.

Tammy spent countless hours talking with me, and she and Ron called me often to see if I was getting along okay. They invited me over for visits, took me out to eat, and generally tried everything that good friends do, but nothing seemed to help. Each day as I left for work, I would wonder how much more of this I could take—the grind, the depression, and the feelings of loss.

Things finally reached a point where I thought that the only possible solution was suicide. It seemed the only way to free myself of all of the pressure. Constantly in my mind was the thought that life from this point on would always be a struggle for my family and me. I was unable to provide for them. I was unorganized in my thoughts and in my actions. I could do nothing more to improve my situation and no one else could either. I was tired and I only wanted to rest. The longer I thought about it, the more suicide seemed like the best answer. In fact, I thought it was the only answer. It is difficult to describe or even imagine now how I was thinking, not even giving thoughts to how this action might affect my children's lives.

Adding to my tormented thoughts were memories of my father's sudden death the year before. I had been very close to him, and I had always turned to him first during my times of trouble. He had been diagnosed with terminal colon cancer, but he chose not to tell the family. He wanted to spare us the heartache of watching him suffer and slowly die. My family and I had no idea that he would live for only a few short months.

On July 1, 1980, he committed suicide. This came as a terrible shock to all of us. He had always provided for me; my mom; my sister, Paula; and my brother, Alan. We were left trying to pick up the pieces and put them back together again. My father had been a strong foundation that we all had counted on for support. His family had always been very important to him. In addition to being the bread-winner for all of us, he would schedule regular get-togethers, for which he would cook too much food and make us eat until we could hardly move. He always made time to give us the opportunity to sit around and share each other's company.

Now he was gone, and the security I had drawn from my father's love and strength was no longer within reach. The sudden loss was probably worse for us than if we had been forced to watch him slowly die of cancer. At least then we might have been prepared and have been able to make our peace beforehand. Instead, he left us without the close goodbyes we might have had. He made peace with himself and ended his life. Now I felt as if I needed to do the same. Death was the only thing that I felt could make me truly free. I was lost and desperate. Once I even tried to end it all by jumping out of a car that was traveling at 75 mph. The pressures had become more than I could handle. Just when I was at the end and ready to take that final step, something happened. I can clearly remember that day even now. The thoughts, the feelings, the smells, and the visions are crystal clear to me.

I awoke one morning in late May to the sound of my alarm clock blaring in my ear. It was six o'clock, and another long, colorless day of depression was ahead of me. The thought of getting out of bed was unbearable. I only wanted to stay covered up and hidden from the pain, but eventually I got out of bed. Feeling heavy with stress, I dragged myself into my private bathroom and into the shower. My bathroom was beautiful. As I walked in, the long marble-topped vanity with his-and-hers sinks was on the left, and the toilet and the frosted-glass shower followed. Directly across from the shower was a glorious garden tub so big that I could lose myself in it and leave the world behind. In front of the tub was a walk-in closet big enough to be a sitting room. As I took a long, hot shower, I hoped I could wash away all of the aches and pains that I felt, but nothing could remove the strongest pain of all, which was in my heart. I begrudgingly dressed in silence, dreading the day ahead.

That morning, my first appointment was scheduled with a customer in Johnstown, Pennsylvania, to meet about my line of cards. Once I was ready, I quietly peeked into the bedrooms and checked on Tina and Geoff, as I did every morning before I left for work. This routine was my salvation and comfort, along with having my mom living with us. Although Mom and I never saw eye to eye in the past, she was making up for it now. It was a big sacrifice for her to leave her home and move in with us, but I believe it also helped her adjust to not having Dad around anymore. I left the house that morning in sadness, trying to prepare myself to face the world one more day.

The two-hour drive to Johnstown was a bit dreadful, as I had feared, even though it was a beautiful day. I remember how my depressing thoughts were so ironic when the spring day was so lovely.

Spring was a time for hope, but my life was crumbling down around me. I was looking for someone to blame, and I blamed myself. I looked back over the rubble that had been my life, and I could see specific points where I had failed. I felt guilty, ugly, and small. My self-esteem was so low that I was sure that no one would ever love me again. In my state of my mind, I did not feel worthy of being loved. Feeling physically ill with guilt, I drove in silence.

The scenery flew by me without my noticing any of it, though in the past I relished these drives where I could observe the country scenes. Instead, my mind was seeing the world through my heavy thoughts. I wondered if I would ever find happiness again. I was sure that I would not. I felt destined to be an unhappy, unloved shell of a person. Then I realized the worst part of all—I had completely forgotten how it felt to be loved. My mom and my kids loved me, but somehow it did not seem to be enough. I felt so incredibly empty. My rollercoaster mind remembered the highs of being loved and the lows of feeling depressed.

Once again, I thought about death. I wondered how Tina and Geoff would get along without me. I knew my mom would care for them, maybe even better than I could. I wished my life would end right then and there, that some force would come down and drain the life out of my body and take me away. There seemed to be no reason for me to live if there was no purpose. I was going nowhere and I was all alone.

The longer I drove, the more the pressure seemed to consume me. My stomach felt tight, and a painful fire tore through my midsection. I began to feel even more depressed and uncomfortable as I neared Johnstown. My mind began to feel numb, and I had difficulty trying to think logically. With what little energy I had left, I screamed, "God, why must I go on? Why, why?"

This was it. The dam had broken. I felt like my life was being taken away in the flood of grief. I had finally reached the end that Tammy had warned me about. I started to cry. I continued down the long, windy mountain to the valley where Johnstown was located. Trees covered the two-lane road like an ongoing tunnel. Scared and shaking, with tears running down my cheeks, I was confused and could no longer think clearly. I felt as if I were a ghost in the land of the living and that no one could see or notice me. Perhaps I was a nonperson. I was doing nothing more than going through the motions of life and not really living it fully. Nothing had meaning, and meaning meant nothing. It was not long before desperation gripped me once again.

The road was narrow and maybe a little dangerous for someone like me who was unfamiliar with the area. Again, I began to cry out to God. "Dear God, why must I go on?" My wish was to die. Being relieved of the emotional scars of life had to be better than what I was enduring. Why did I have to go through so much alone? What terrible thing had I done to deserve so much pain and so many problems? "If You have a purpose for my life, then why can't You show me?" I yelled. Immediately, I felt a strong shooting pain throughout my hand. I had been pounding my fist on the dashboard over and over out of anger without an awareness of my actions. The tears came even faster now than they had before. My vision was blurred. I thought I would lose control of my car. That would free me of my pain, so maybe it wasn't such a bad idea; it would all be over then.

I had to pull myself together. I was almost in Johnstown, and I had a job to do there. More sanely, I fought to focus on the job I had to do and on my family. I began to regain control and felt a penetrating warmth run through my body. It was the first feeling other than complete exhaustion and the desire to give up that I had felt in a long time. This warm feeling not only ran through my stomach and my chest but from the top of my head down to my feet, making me completely relaxed. It freed me from all the tension I had felt before. It was a wonderful feeling! This tingling sensation did not leave me right away; it gave me a sense that a strong flood of love was washing over me. I was astounded. Soon I began to realize that all of my feelings of pain were gone, replaced by a sense of complete and total peace in my mind, my body, and my soul.

What was this feeling and where had it come from? Had something physically happened to my body because of all of the strain I had been under? Then I realized that the tears that had been pouring down my face had stopped as quickly as they had started. My eyes were completely dry; the tears were all gone. I knew that on the outside, I still looked the same. Nothing about my appearance had changed, but on the inside, I was different. I knew it. There was some sort of presence with me—a heavenly presence.

The whole experience of that glorious feeling washing over me and filling me with love felt like it took less than half an hour. I looked down at my watch and realized that almost two hours had passed—two whole hours of intense feelings. When the experience started, I had found myself driving on out-of-the-way streets, almost as if I was guided to do so. It would make me late for my appointment, but somehow, I didn't care. Something more important was happening, better than making another sale or meeting a new client. In my mind, I could hear a voice saying to me, *I love you, Nora Ann. Can you hear Me? I love you, Nora Ann. I love you, My child.*

Was I telling this to myself, or was it someone or something else? Then it struck me. It could not be me talking; I hated myself. I would never have said those things. It had to be from another power—a power higher than myself.

Once I accepted that this power was speaking to me, I did my best to keep my mind open so that I could more clearly understand what was being said so I could etch it into my memory. The message coming to me was about my father and his death. The voice assured me that my dad was there by His side. He used Scriptures to explain how my father had made his way into heaven, even though he had committed suicide. The verse used was from Revelations 3:20

(NIV), "I stand at the door and knock; if any man hears My voice and opens the door; I will come in and eat with him, and he with Me." It had been a great comfort to me that my father had asked the Lord into his life several weeks before he died.

The Scripture reassured me that even though he had taken his own life, he was still able to see God and to live with Him in glory. The voice I heard assured me my father was with God. He explained that my dad was like a new babe. He was a brand-new Christian with a brand-new beginning. He had no time to learn that it was against God's will to take his life, so his innocence had saved him from eternal damnation.

As I continued my drive, the experience seemed to go on and on. The longer it lasted, the stronger my impression was that there was a presence with me in the car. It was the presence of God that I felt next to me—comforting me and letting me know how very much He cared. His presence was even stronger as my experience continued. It was almost as if I could reach across the seat and touch Him. I recall sliding my hand over the passenger seat as if to feel some-one there. It may sound absurd, but I had to know. I could not actually feel him as another human person, but I felt a warm power that reassured me that, yes, He was there. I knew then that all of the feelings that I had been experiencing were as right and as pure as could be.

Throughout the experience, I had the feeling that I could laugh (for the first time in weeks), talk, and cry for the goodness of the spirit in our hearts. It was a feeling of fullness, a feeling that everything would be okay and everything would work out. I was not alone anymore, because God was there with me. He loved me and He had a plan for me. I also recall that, as the spiritual awareness went on, I felt oddly disjointed, almost as if I were out of body. I felt as though I was no longer at the controls. I was on some sort of autopilot. My body moved to shift gears, to brake, and to turn the steering wheel, but there was no conscious effort to do so.

The strange part about all of this is that I had no fear. I felt protected. It was as if the entire car were wrapped up in some sort of bubble and nothing could penetrate it or hurt me. The intensity of the fullness and contentment I felt was so energizing that it was difficult to explain. Words never seem to be enough to help others understand how uplifting it was to be freed from my burdens and stress. My inner self was healing and optimistic, comforted by the experience of learning about His love for me.

Try to imagine a point in your life when you felt optimistic about everything. You had no worries, no immediate responsibilities, and everything was going your way. Remember how bright and new everything seemed to be. Take that feeling and double it. The feelings were light and bright. My sense of direction was sure. I was safe, and I was saved. Everything before this was painful and full of grief, but now I finally felt as if everything was okay. Even today, every time I think back to my "spiritual awakening," I can clearly remember those emotions. If I feel myself spiraling down, I remember that day. This pulls me through the rough spots and helps me to move forward peacefully.

Chapter 2

I finally arrived in Johnstown and found the card and gift shop. Now I was a different person with a new point of view. For a while in the store, I wondered if anyone there could see something different about me. Of course, I finally realized they wouldn't, because they had never seen me before. The difference was within me. I was preoccupied and oblivious to what was happening around me. I was walking on air. It was too good to be true. I was barely able to contain the joy I felt, but I managed to take care of business. Unlike my working days in the past, the day was full with my seeing the humor in things and feelings of benevolence toward people. I purposely made eye contact with everyone I saw. I said hello as a way of letting them know that all was right with the world.

When I returned home that evening, I realized that the day had gone by fast. Before the awakening, I would come home tired and withdrawn after being beaten down by the world. This time, instead of withdrawing to my room in a depressed mood, I felt full of happiness and energy. Nevertheless, my mind was questioning how I could possibly have had such a wonderful experience and a new sense of self-worth. One of the biggest concerns I had was sort of a reality check. What had truly happened? Was it real or just something my overstressed mind had produced? I thought back to traveling those country roads and listening to His voice. I knew the spirit and power behind those words were real, and I knew that the feeling in those words was much more than I could produce myself through any conscious or subconscious effort.

One of the best revelations that came out of this experience was that we have a freedom of choice in all things. I, like many others, had been choosing the easy, popular way to live, the wider gate that is easy to walk through. I had been looking for answers among the modern lifestyle of choosing things over belief. Because of my choices, the results were scarring, painful, hurtful, and—if I had gone ahead with suicide—potentially terminal. For whatever reason, God revealed the answer to my prayers, and I embraced the option He offered. His one choice for us is the narrow gate. That decision to accept Jesus into my life and follow the path He laid out before me through the "narrow gate" made a colossal difference in my life then and now.

Another revelation God has shown me through His love is that I was not as bad of a person as I had thought. He gave me reassurance that I was not a failure. He has shown me that there is hope and there is a future.

The day in Johnstown had gone so well that I was not sure I wanted to sleep that night. Because I was wound up and wanted to stay close to that feeling He had given to me, I was afraid to sleep—afraid it would all be lost. Perhaps I still was not convinced that it had really happened. I wanted to be sure of that closeness and oneness with the Spirit of God. I wanted to know without any doubt how much I was loved, the deepest emotions of love from the ultimate giver of love.

Over the years, I have come to realize that it is a precious gift to be loved and to be able to give love to another. Through all of my troubles, during the time of my divorce and the rough times since then, I have come to know that God's love carries me through everything I have come up against. We are all loved unconditionally, if we will just reach out and accept it. Jesus died for us so that we could be set free from our shortcomings and overcome the problems that we make for ourselves. It was so comforting and reassuring to be able to communicate with the Lord—to talk, to think, to be heard, to get answers. I realized that my life was not beyond repair. He showed me that my life as it had been needed a little bit of cleaning up and maintenance. Then I could begin to move forward again. God is the ultimate mechanic, and we are His labor of love.

Throughout my hardships, He showed me how much He loved me. There is no doubt that He loves me even more than I could ever love my own children. God's capacity to love is awesome. With warm thoughts like these, I was finally able to sleep a peaceful sleep for the first time in months.

The next morning came early, and when I woke up, the sun was already peeking through the curtains. I lay there and felt the sun on my face. Suddenly, I sat bolt upright. Had the day before been a dream? Did I really have a life-changing encounter with the Spirit?

I decided that what I had experienced had been real. Inside, I could still feel the electricity from God jolting me back into life. It was like a spiritual hangover. As the reality of my experience washed over me, I felt lifted emotionally and I experienced the overwhelming optimism that had driven me through the day before.

Then I thought, I can't keep this feeling to myself any longer. I've got to share this or I'll burst. The only problem was deciding with whom to share this. Who would believe it? Soon I found myself on the floor next to my bed, doing something I had not done in years. I was kneeling to pray.

"Dear Father in heaven," I started. "I know You are real, loving me so much." At that point, I remember the tears, not from sadness this time but from fullness of joy, as they rolled down my cheeks. "I want to know You better. I said the prayer of faith years ago, but I am asking You again to come into my life. Forgive me my sins and help me to be what You would have me be. Guide me through my life in all things." When I finished praying, I felt as though the Lord's arms were around me. I felt an incredible feeling of comfort as I sat on the floor beside my bed. Tears of joy and cleansing—warm tears that seemed as if they came right from my soul—streamed down my face. I was being cleansed from the inside out. My tears made me feel like a rainbow following a spring shower.

Chapter 3

*A*s He cleansed and renewed me, I marveled at how He was beginning to make me a new person. Though it was an exciting time for me personally, I had to share the Lord's work in me, but with whom? I was not sure that I should just share this with my family. They knew about the stress I had been under before this happened, and I wasn't sure they would accept this great news for what it was. Although it was certainly a wonderful experience, it could bring about an unexpected and unpleasant response during trying times.

The excitement was overwhelming, and I felt the need to share it with someone before I burst. I decided to call Tammy, and while we were on the phone before telling her my story, I asked her if she and Ron were trying to adopt a baby. She was completely shocked by my question. There was a long period of silence before she said that they were. She wondered how I had known since they had not told anyone of their intentions. I then began to explain what had happened to me the day before.

Tammy was fascinated by my spiritual experience. She listened for a long time, amazed at how I had come to know their secret. The Lord had given me the knowledge of their desire to adopt so that I could use that information to tell her about Him. The Lord had given me a gift of wisdom, similar to prophecy, but not quite the same. I had knowledge of some future events whose outcome no one else could possibly foresee. He impressed upon my mind the knowledge of future events. I knew that before Tammy and Ron ever finalized their adoption efforts that Tammy would become pregnant with a son. That is exactly what happened, except that now they have two sons. This gift was the beginning of a new understanding between the Lord and me. I was hesitant about using it, but He showed me the way. I could never have imagined what plans He would reveal to me.

Tammy didn't know the Lord yet, but apparently our regular talks about the Lord had some effect on her. In her early years, Tammy had dealt with much loss. Her father died of an aneurysm when she was eleven. Her mother died from alcoholism when Tammy was in her early twenties. Her brother also became an alcoholic, affected by all of the problems associated with it. Mrs. Heiser, the woman who became her proxy mother, also died, and as time passed, Tammy lost her in-laws as well. Other than her husband, there was no one for her to share her life with, except me, her best friend. I'd like to think that I was responsible for planting the seed of Tammy's spiritual growth.

After I later moved from Pennsylvania to Ohio, I continued to pray for Tammy and Ron. She came to know the Lord and found how He could spiritually change a person's outlook. Ron was already a Christian, and through our regular conversations with Tammy about the Lord, we helped her to open up to His special love. She now looks at all aspects of her life differently than before. She has found new meaning and fulfillment to help her overcome the dark days of depression that had been a big part of her life for many years.

The positive and patient response from Tammy encouraged me to share my newfound faith with others as well. I still felt an incredible urge to spread the word about what God had done for me. The joy of faith and the certainty that He brought continued to motivate me. A new thought started working in my mind—the idea that He would move me somewhere far away from where I was. At first, I thought that maybe this feeling was a by-product of the experience, but the restlessness did not cease. It kept hammering at me in my conscious moments.

I decided to share God with my good friends Terry and Pat. I had come to know them after they bought an acre of property from the land that my husband and I had owned. We had known each other for a long time, and they were very caring people. I can recall many times when money was tight, especially around the holidays, they would bring us bags of groceries to help us get through rough spots. I didn't realize at that time how God was working through them to provide for us, but later it became clear that He had been watching and waiting on me.

Terry and Pat were the kind of people who never grew tired of giving. They even gave to my sweet tooth. Anyone who knows me at all knows how weak I am when it comes to sweets. Whenever I was feeling down, Terry would bring over a delicious apple cake, and my mood was always lifted. Pat even came over to cut the grass for me. They were always there and continued to give in many ways. Their encouragement alone was a tremendous help. Sharing my conversion with them was a chance for me to offer them encouragement about the precious love that God has to offer for all of us.

The day after my experience, I sat having tea in Pat and Terry's home. I tried to explain what I experienced the previous day. The words couldn't match my feelings, but Terry and Pat soon understood. They began asking questions and they were as much in awe of the work that God had done through me as I was. I was beginning to enjoy this new experience of sharing, one of the ways God works through us in order to accomplish things. I even expressed my thoughts to Terry and Pat that I felt that I may be moving.

Pat quickly blurted out, "How can you be sure it was really God speaking to you? Why would He even want you to leave when your family and friends are all here?"

Terry answered, "Pat's right, you wouldn't want to move that far away and later decide it was a mistake. You know we love you and want you to be happy, but you won't have anyone close by to help you if you need them. Please give this more thought before you make your final decision."

"If you really believe this is what you are supposed to do, then I guess God will take care of you," Pat replied. "We just don't think it's a good idea for you to leave and be on your own with two kids."

It was obvious that Terry and Pat did not associate me leaving with it being a message from God. They didn't think it seemed natural for God to ask me to give up everything and follow Him to another state. We had been friends for years and grown very close. It would be very difficult to leave them and all my family and friends I loved so much. In all honesty, I was terrified to move away. My emotions ran rampant when I heard this message, and I too questioned it. Like it or not, I knew it was that still, soft voice of the Lord himself which spoke to me.

Ever since those early days when I heard the Spirit of the Lord, I have learned that God doesn't always ask us to do things that seem natural or easy for us. Often, He asks us to do things that may not even make sense to us at the time. Before taking a leap of faith, pray about it continuously until you have your answer. Never allow yourself to be deceived. The best suggestion I can offer is to read your Bible.

The Word of God is alive today just as it was hundreds of years ago. The Bible is God-breathed. It was He who inspired the saints to write the books of the Bible in the beginning.

Chapter 4

The feeling that God was ready to work some great feat in my life never went away. Daily I received the impression that I was to move, and it grew stronger and stronger. The more that feeling grew, the more clouded my mind became. It seemed that God did not seem quite as clear or simple to me anymore.

Why would He uproot me so soon? Why was I going away from the people and things I had grown so comfortable with over the years? What plans did He have for me? My mind was swimming with all kinds of thoughts that seemed scary and impossible to me. How could I move away and start over when I was just starting to put things together here? Good question. All I knew was that I felt led to make some sort of decision very soon.

One Friday afternoon, several months after my experience, I was at home updating some paperwork for my job when the thought of a move started to begin to work heavily on my mind. Setting aside my work, I took my Bible into my hands and began reading. Whenever I felt lost for answers, I found that reading Scripture pointed me in the right direction. At first, the words seemed blurred and meaningless to me. Then an inner peace came over me and it became clear. I had to go to church the next morning to get some sort of confirmation about the decision I needed to make.

The next morning, I was up at5:30 a.m. It was easy for me to get up because of all of the excitement that was running through my body. This was the day my future would be laid out before me. Dressing quickly, I quietly went past the children's rooms so I wouldn't awaken them. I am sure my mother heard me leave, but she never questioned where I had to go or what I had to do. This morning, the Spirit was leading me, and I had to go.

Once in the garage, I looked outside to see that it had snowed about two inches during the night and more was on the way. It was still coming down very hard. Since Pennsylvania snowstorms can be very dangerous, I wondered if I should go or not. Then I decided that if it was God's will for me to be at the 6:00 a.m. service, then I had to go, no matter what. Once I had backed the car out of the garage and entered the slippery roads, I also noticed how poor the visibility was. It was scary to be driving on these icy country roads, but I prayed that I would get there safely. My prayers were answered when I pulled into the empty parking lot awhile later.

Everything was quiet as I walked up to the front door, opened it, and peered in. Only one person was in the building at the front of the church. I started down the aisle, and about halfway down, I stopped and sat down. As I started to thank God for getting me there safely, I saw someone at the altar who caught my eye.

It was a woman in her late fifties. On the whole, she was plain with dark hair flecked with gray. A scarf covered her head, and she wore a well-worn coat and faded boots. For some reason, I knew I had to go up and kneel beside her. I made my way to the altar and nervously kneeled down beside her. Then I wondered if I should just quietly pray or talk to her. Luckily, the woman broke the ice and started talking to me.

She told me that she regularly attended morning services there, but on this particular day, the service had been canceled due to the weather. She made it a point to be there anyway to pray for a sick member of her family. Then, before I knew what was happening, we were talking like we were long-lost friends. We began to pray together. After about a half hour of quiet praying, the woman stopped and looked at me in a puzzled way. She asked me if I would do the Stations of the Cross with her, so I agreed.

We prayed at each one. When we stopped at the one where Jesus falls with His cross, she looked me straight in the eye, and said, "You need to make a very big decision, so pick up your cross and go, don't look back. Just go! Wherever it is, don't be afraid. You don't need to worry, because I can feel that everything will be okay."

I was stunned. It was as if the woman was an angel sent to guide me on a journey that would take me far away. Suddenly, my need to be at the church was revealed and definite. My answer had come. I was going to move. I was stunned as I watched her leave within seconds after she told me to move and not look back. I followed her out, but when I got outside, she was gone. At that point, I got back in the car and left. I couldn't get past what just happened, but I knew I was, without a doubt, moving to Ohio.

Chapter 5

*B*eing the good friends that they are, Tammy, Terry, and Pat accepted the news of my move as well as could be expected. Tammy needed reassuring that I would keep in touch and that we would always remain friends. Terry and Pat pitched in any way that they could to help me prepare for God's adventure. Tina, Geoff, and I would stay in our home until the school year was over. Mom was finally doing better emotionally, and being with her grandchildren did her a world of good. She was ready to get on with her life. Soon it would be time for her to prepare to leave as well. I would continue to look for guidance as to exactly where my work would take me and where God planned to move us. I knew it would be an adventure, because that was the way my life had been with God up until that point.

I could not believe how He was healing me, helping me grow, and maturing me. Naturally, I had trouble always accepting the parts of His plan for my life that He had revealed to me. God told me that I would travel around Ohio and there I would meet a man who would help me build a church. That part sounded good to me. Also, this man would love me more than any man can. Then came the rest of the message.

Thinking about it even now gives me a feeling of peace, because I had no idea what He had told me was supposed to mean. I was told that the prison ministries and halfway houses, as well as my birthday, would be an important factor in my new life. Also, I received the message that there would be a lot more heartache and heartbreak before me in Ohio, but if I remained faithful to Him, He would pull me through it, and I would be a better person for it.

As my days in Pennsylvania grew fewer, I remember times that I had feelings of doubt that brought fear and indescribable emptiness. I felt like I was left alone in an empty, dark place with nothing to touch but slippery walls and no one to talk to except myself. At the time, I did not understand the isolation, but now I know that the emptiness we sometimes feel is a sign of God rearranging something in our lives.

Sometimes moving out of a house or an apartment that you have lived in for a while gives you a sense of grief as you walk through the dwelling for the last time and realize you will never be back. I walked through my house and remembered the special people with whom I had shared memories. Despite my beautiful reflections of the past, I still only felt emptiness. My emotional home was being packed up and moved by the Lord, leaving me with empty rooms and pale memories until life planted me in a new place.

The beautiful part about being one with God is how He can turn things around. Instead of continuing to feel empty and depressed about the move, He soon turned those emotions into feelings of peace, joy, and a sense of purpose. Even though moving was difficult emotionally and physically, I knew I would have my best friend with me. Jesus had become my foundation, and in those difficult days, I leaned on Him heavily. His support was always there. It was truly a blessing how my faith blossomed in those days. Prayer, trust, and meditation on His words helped me through every part of the move. I had faith that He would help me find everything in life that I needed. In retrospect, that has continued to be true.

One of my last great memories of Pennsylvania happened near Christmas and illustrates the ever-giving attitude of Jesus. One day, I awoke and felt compelled to go out shopping. I phoned Tammy and convinced her to go with me. Before we reached the store, I clued Tammy into the fact that we were on a mission. She agreed to it and actually took charge. When we arrived at the store, there were rows of fresh flowers in the doorway, and their scent reminded me that spring could not be far away, whether it was the seasonal spring or the spring of my new life. I felt that a basket of fresh rainbow-colored flowers would make the best arrangement for our "mission." I knew, however, that I was to allow Tammy to pick whatever flowers she felt were right.

Tammy convinced me to buy a poinsettia, although I really only wanted a basket of fresh flowers. I bought the plant reluctantly and had it wrapped in brown paper and left the store, with the intent of accomplishing our mission. On the way home, we deliberately took the long way so that we would pass a certain gas station near West Newton that was run by a woman we knew as Madge. We knew little about

Madge except that she had lost her husband about a year before and that she lived with her grandson in a small trailer across the street from the gas station. We knew she was having financial difficulties. Her husband had distrusted American banks, so he hid their life savings in a place only he knew. When he died, the secret died with him. This worried Madge to no end as she struggled to take care of her grandson and herself.

Tammy and I marched into the station and found Madge behind the cooler. We talked a little bit, and then I told her what God had told me in my prayers that morning. He had told me that it was my responsibility to get a message to Madge. He wanted her to know that He was watching out for her and loved her very much. After I finished telling this to Madge, I pulled the wrapper off of the poinsettia and told her that the flower was hers as a symbol of God's words to her. She looked at both of us for a second and then began to cry. After she pulled her emotions together, she told us of a conversation she had had with her grandson just five minutes before we arrived. He had asked her what she would want for Christmas if she could have anything. She told him that she would want a poinsettia because this plant had been a part of the holiday tradition that she and her husband had shared for years. Then she told me how she had given up hope of having a merry Christmas because they had no money for gifts.

When Tammy and I left her and her grandson, there were smiles on their faces. We were filled with a wonderful feeling. We were glad that we had been obedient and had followed God's morning message to me. There is no greater reward than to know that you have been obedient to the Spirit. The knowledge of that obedience creates a deep awareness of how God works in you and helps you to recognize His voice above the din of all of the other voices that surround us and compete for our attention. That makes your path easier to see as well as to follow.

Psalms 32:8 (NIV) says, "I will instruct you and teach you in the way you should go; I will counsel you and watch over you." God was indeed guiding me and teaching me. I just had to remember to let my own beliefs stay out of the way so that I could let His wishes be the ones to follow. God is faithful to what He says He will do, and He is also faithful to give to those like Madge who need it, often by working through and with others who are following His ways.

Chapter 6

*A*fter it became clear to me that He was going to move me spiritually, I found God forcing me to rely on Him more and more, instead of finding answers like I had in my old comfort zones. I was being uprooted, and He wanted me to be ready. Still waiting for a clear direction of just where and when we would move, I could feel that it would be soon. I finally received a hint.

The answers became clear to me one day when I was working at the information center on the first day of the trade show at the Expo Mart in Monroeville, Pennsylvania. Somehow, I knew the next link to my future job was about to take place. I knew there was an answer waiting for me. At the show, I noticed a new product line called Oceans West. They were in need of a representative for their eastern Ohio and western Pennsylvania territory. Jordache was also hiring, and a representative from that company called and left a message for me to call them. I interviewed with both companies, and they both seemed to go well. However, the Jordache representative gave me the impression that he was looking for a man to fill the position. The Oceans West possibility was a little stronger. In the meantime, I prayed to the Lord that He would guide me to the job that He wanted me to have so that I could best reach His goal for my life.

I believe that God gave me a good friend to help me at this time of uncertainty. Ginger was from New York, and I had known her for about two years through my shoe modeling. At one of the shows where we had both been modeling, she stayed with me to save a few dollars on lodging. She was strong in the faith and was very interested in my story about the things God was doing in my life. After the trade show in Monroeville was over, Ginger came over to my house one evening. We felt led to pray and ask God to open wide the doors to my future so I could make the decisions He would reveal to me. We asked Him to give His direction for my life, especially when it involved work. We also prayed that He would close doors that had been opened in the past that had hindered my spiritual growth. A faithful follower, Ginger was so understanding and giving that I could not help but be encouraged in the good things that were going to come soon.

That magical night (there is no other way to describe it), Ginger told me she not only felt led to pray with me about my future, but she also talked to me about praying for the gift of tongues. She must have been in tune with the Spirit, since it was not long before I felt the Lord telling me to pray for the gift of developing a spiritual prayer language. I never did succeed at the time, but I thought about Ginger and how special it was that she had this gift. Not everyone has to have this gift in order to be in communication with God.

Less than forty-eight hours after praying with Ginger about the future, I received a call from the Jordache Shoe Corporation in New York City. They wanted me to fly in for a second interview. That same day, Ocean West called. They offered me the job of representing them in the new territory. I told them I would need a few days to decide. Then Ginger and I made plans to fly to New York. We arrived on Wednesday and my interview was not until Thursday. Ginger returned the favor of letting me stay at her place. She knew I was really nervous, but again the

Lord was guiding her to help me. She knew exactly what to do to keep me calm and confident.

Ginger and her boyfriend, Scott, took me out to dinner and then to an evening Bible study at a nearby Lutheran church. The church was a large, old, imposing structure that did not look friendly from the outside, but the inside was what really mattered, and it made a difference for me. There were about seventy people there as well as a guest speaker that Ginger and Scott said was very good. To be honest, I do not remember much about the speaker, because the Spirit went to work on me as soon as I walked through the door.

We sat down and I started meditating in prayer immediately. I was deep in prayer when I felt this strange sort of energy start to run from my feet to my head. Then the voice of the speaker seamed to get quieter and quieter. I felt as if I was being removed from the people in the church. I was apart from them. I was in the gathering, but I wasn't a part of it. God was up to something. In this separated state, I asked the Lord again for the gift of tongues and I sat quietly as the muffled noises around me droned on. I was able to hear that still, small voice that was God's Spirit speaking to me.

What I was hearing was that I had to make a choice between the two jobs right away (and that was news to me, because I hadn't even been offered the Jordache position yet), and that would be my choice to make. This was the situation: Oceans West had offered me the job in western Pennsylvania and eastern Ohio. I was told that Jordache would be offering me a position to represent them in Virginia, West Virginia, and western Pennsylvania. Taking that job would mean that I would probably miss God's will for my life, because I was sure that He told me Ohio was where I was supposed to be. The voice told me that I would do well at either job and would be rewarded for my hard work no matter which position I chose.

I was confused. When the voice stopped, I found myself praying, and praying hard. I started to slip back into the here and now a bit at a time. When I became aware of what I was saying, it was totally beyond me. The words were all new to me, and they just poured from my mouth. The Lord had given me my prayer language. It electrified me more and made me resolve with even more seriousness to do His will. Not long after my divine experience, I was restored back to the present to find the service had ended, and we headed out to the car. Once we got into the car,

Ginger turned to me and asked if what she heard me saying during the service was me praying in tongues. I told her that it was, and the three of us praised God all the way home!

Chapter 7

I believe that my prayers that night in late 1984 helped me to become more resolved about my decision to move. I was no longer nervous, and I followed through with the interview with Oceans West. I accepted the job to work in a new territory selling an undeveloped line of shoes. With relatively no clients and a new product line, I knew I had a lot of work ahead of me, but I jumped into it wholeheartedly. Of course, we were still at home in Pennsylvania and I would travel on short trips for a while until things became clear. Knowing that God wanted me to move was somehow part of the whole new plan.

I preset appointments for my first day of work with Oceans West in Cleveland, Ohio, at the May Company, and in Akron at O'Neal's. I woke up at 4:00 a.m.in complete darkness, prayed, showered, and looked in on my children, Tina and Geoff. Then

I quickly went down to the garage, got into my car, and drove away so that I could get an early start on my day. There was a long drive ahead of me before my working day would even begin. That drive was nothing short of amazing.

To describe it as being Spirit-filled would be accurate, but it was more than that. It was motivational, enlightening, educational, and exciting. For most of the drive, I concentrated on prayer and meditation. Then I put on tapes of Amy Grant, Debbie Boone, and Kenneth Copeland, and sang along with them to lift my spirits. Several hours into my drive, I felt incredibly consumed with His Spirit. I felt this way not only because He had come into my life, but also because He had promised me He would show me how to live. This was not just an average business trip to sell shoes. This trip was engineered by God to help me find His purpose for my life.

I had planned on making this trip an overnighter, which most sales representatives who travel will tell you is somewhat out of the ordinary for having only two stops. Normally, the key is to balance accounts so that they will fully compensate travel expenses. As I said before, this was not an average trip. I felt I should trust in the Lord to provide for all my needs. If He allowed me to make enough sales to merit an overnight trip, fine. If not, I was sure that He would take care of me. This trip was a mission.

When I reached the Akron area, I was well ahead of schedule, so I decided to stop, get a room, and relax for a while. I found the Holiday Inn at Routes 77 and 18 in Fairlawn. It was there that I began to become aware of God watching over me. Because of a car accident years before, my back had been bothering me, and I had been thinking how lucky I would be if I found a room with a waterbed. The desk clerk told me they had no more single rooms available, but she called the Holiday Inn at Strongsville. When I was checking in at this second motel, the clerk handed me the key, then suddenly pulled her hand back and asked, "Would you like a room with a waterbed?" and I thought to myself, *Praise God!* As I walked back to my car, I had the widest grin on my face. He was there, and He was listening to my thoughts. I thanked Him for being with me on this adventure.

No one knows us better than the Lord. He made us and He knows what each of us is about. I always try to remember to let Him work in my life in His way, and things have an uncanny way of working out. Many times, however, we stand in His way. We just need to accept the fact that no matter what we think or know, God is there waiting for us to turn to Him. Then, and only then, He will take care of our needs.

After resting in the room for a short while, I organized my sales materials and went to O'Neil's. My head was swimming with so many things related to God that I could hardly concentrate on my presentation, but God took care of that. The line of shoes was fashionable, exciting, and virtually sold itself. I was there for a couple of hours and had the full attention of two buyers for the store.

They were receptive to my presentation and ordered a lot of shoes. Once again, He had provided for me. As I left the store, it was almost noon, so I decided to use my extra time to drive through the country on the west side of Akron.

As I drove, I remembered several things that the Lord had told me shortly after I was saved. One thought was that I would build a church somewhere in Northeastern Ohio. I figured the open spaces west of Akron would be as good a place as any, so I began looking for a building location. He had also told me that I would meet a man in Ohio who would help me to build a church and that this man would love me deeply. I had no idea how this church was to be built, but this was what God had told me to do. I thought I should set my sights on doing it as well as I could.

Driving out of the city on Route 18, I prayed a lot and listened to the Spirit. I praised God aloud so that He knew I was grateful to Him for all He had done for me and to let Him know that I was seeking to do His will in my life. God will always guide us best when our motives are in tune with His. I have discovered that when my motives are not quite right—maybe due to selfishness—that my praises do not come easily and they seem to lack conviction and feeling. When this happens, it is time to recheck my reasons for wanting something and bring myself back in harmony with Him.

Somehow on my drive, I was led to a city called Medina, about fifteen miles from Akron. I found myself on a side street near the Friendship Baptist Church. I noticed open land behind the church, so I thought that it would be a good place to start. Two cars were parked in the lot, so I wandered up to the door and knocked. I wondered what the people inside would think of me. What would I say? How about, "Excuse me, you have no idea who I am, but

I'm here to buy the land behind your church to build another church." Or maybe, "Hi! The Lord sent me on a mission to find a place to build a church. Can you help me?" All I could think of as I waited at the door was that they might call the police or a hospital to report an out-of-control woman on the loose in their town. As usual, my imagination was getting the best of me.

Soon, a woman in her mid-twenties came to the door. I asked her about the land behind the church. She was very friendly and helped me as much as she could. After a few words, she invited me inside. She told me that she and the other woman had come to the church to take care of a few things for their Sunday school classes—the Lord at work again. After talking for a while, I told them how I had felt impelled to come to their church for a reason. They still had not turned me over to any authorities, so I decided it was safe to go on with my story.

I told them that God wanted me to build His church somewhere in that part of Ohio. They listened and were friendly, finally inviting me to return that evening for a guest speaker who was coming to talk about the gift of tongues. I accepted their invitation and left. I was able to handle one more appointment that afternoon at a shoe store in Beachwood, and then I went back to my room to do some more work.

Throughout this time, my mind was filled with spiritual thoughts, but I sold more shoes that week than in any other week in my days of traveling. At the church that evening, I was met by one of the two women who had invited me. She introduced me to an older lady named Dorothy who, I was told, also felt led to build a church. She and I talked for a long while and decided to meet for lunch the following afternoon. Now I knew why God had led me there. His guiding hand could not have been any more apparent in my life than it was on this spiritual trip.

Chapter 8

$\mathcal{A}$s amazing as that first full day in Ohio had been, it paled in comparison to what was to come. That Wednesday, I rose early at the hotel and kneeled to pray for guidance during the day. I was sure that it would be special and wanted to be sure that I was fully aware of the things He wanted me to experience and see. As I prayed, a Scripture passage came to mind.

> Remember the former things of old; for I am God, and there is none else; I am God, and there is none like me. Declaring the end from the beginning and from ancient times the things that are not yet done, saying, my counsel shall stand, and I will do all my

pleasure: Calling a ravenous bird from the east, the man that executes my counsel from a far country: yea, I have spoken it, I will also bring it to pass; I have purposed it, I will also do it. Hearken unto me, yea stouthearted, that are far from righteousness; I bring near my righteousness; it shall not be far off, and my salvation shall not tarry: and I will place salvation in Zion for Israel my glory. (Isaiah 46:9–13 KJV)

Then this thought came into my mind: *Go and meet the man named John and he will help to build your church.* That was a major mind-blower for me—another one of those messages that I had been given right after my encounter with God's Spirit about a year before. The promise had been given to me that I would meet a special man and that halfway houses and prison ministries would play a big role in my mission. They would be a key point in my life for a while. I had not known what that meant when I first was given this message, and I did not know now, but I would soon learn.

I was curious about this John that I was supposed to meet. How was I supposed to tell him apart from the millions of other men in the area? I asked God to tell me John's last name. All I could sense was, *Just John. That is all you need to know.* I also had the feeling that my birthday would play an important part in this experience. I knew I would understand when the time came.

Let me just take a moment here to say that when God speaks, He does not speak like we speak to each other (or at least He does not speak to me that way). Instead, He is that still, small voice within me that directs me away from wrong and moves me in the right direction. God speaks to all of us—saved and unsaved—about a lot of things every day. The problem is that, with all the noise around us, that still, small voice often gets crowded out. That is why a quiet time each day is important for all of us. We need to take the time to let the Lord speak to us. We have to listen, and then we have to act. If we do, He will faithfully and justly guide us.

When I had finished my morning meditations, I prepared for brunch with Dorothy. She told me that she worked at a non-Christian radio station in Cleveland on Euclid Avenue. The station was in a building that used to be the rectory of a Catholic church. All that was left of the church was the bell tower with the cross on top. I thought that was very appropriate for my purposes.

The location where we were to meet was a part of the decaying city of Cleveland with much depreciation and crime. After parking my car in a fenced-in lot to protect it, I met Dorothy at the station. She told me a little about the church that used to be there, and how it had become a victim of a changing neighborhood. As the older couples died or moved away, church attendance dwindled to almost nothing. The pastor managed to keep the church going by taking in the area's homeless, and they in turn took care of the church grounds. When that priest passed on, the church was closed and vandals "took care" of the church, to the point where it finally had to be torn down.

Dorothy recalled that the church used to have a beautiful old wooden cross in front of the church that remained after the building was torn down, until the vandals got that too. I told her I would like to have a cross like that on the church I was being directed to build. We went to brunch at the Hofbräuhaus and swapped our dreams about church-building. It was an enjoyable time and serves as an example of how God shows us that we are not laboring alone in His work.

Dorothy and I were like old friends, and we chatted for some time before I had to get ready to go to my two o'clock appointment at the downtown May Company. Since we later kept in contact, I learned that Dorothy influenced the radio station managers where she worked to change some of their programming. They had been playing only hard rock, and later they programmed Christian music and talk. She was in the right place at the right time. God puts us in places to do His work, not just to make a living.

Before we parted that day from our enjoyable visit, I told Dorothy about the word I had received to seek out and meet a man named John. She listened politely, but cautioned me about running around Cleveland in search of this "John" fellow. She told me the city was a dangerous place. Dorothy's directions to the May Company, coupled with the guidance I was getting from the Spirit, were an unbeatable combination.

I made my way downtown with no problems and prayed for just a small thing—a parking place. I found one without a problem in the parking area under the courthouse. Once I had parked the car and was back on ground level, I suddenly had a strange feeling. A combination of nervousness, fear, and joy—it was like the mixture of having a birthday party, getting a speeding ticket, and having a big job interview all in one. It was just strange, and I wondered if maybe I should take Dorothy's advice and head back to the car. Instead, I pressed on through these unusual feelings with the anticipation that today, somehow, in some way, I was going to meet someone named John.

Since it took less time than I thought to get downtown from the restaurant, I decided to go to the park above. The day was exceptionally warm for mid-October, and I left my coat in the car. I was dressed in my favorite teal-blue business suit, which meant I was overdressed for the park. The park overlooking Lake Erie was relatively empty with only two people there. To my right as I faced the lake, there was a man sitting in his pickup truck eating his lunch. The other was a man leaning on a brick wall overlooking Lake Erie, apparently searching for something. Neither looked my way, nor did they look like the "John" person I expected to meet. I still had the feeling that I was where I was supposed to be.

I stood there wondering what to do and I felt that I should learn more about the man staring at the lake. The only place I could go was to the same area where the man was and stand next to him, but he looked a little rough with long, sandy-blond hair pulled back into a ponytail. The Lord would not give me any rest. I was absolutely compelled to go look at the view. There was no way I would not go look at the view and miss God's direction, even though I was not completely comfortable in doing so.

I stood there, closed my eyes, and said a short prayer asking Him to protect me, and, remarkably, I felt safe right away. I was calm and summoned up the courage to move my feet over to the wall. I slowly approached the wall from the farthest point to the right. The man was on the far left, so I focused on the wall and finally arrived at the wall and looked out over the lake. The first thought coming into my mind was that the view was the worst I had ever seen. Looking straight down, there were dirty old train tracks that were full of all kinds of debris. An uninspiring Cleveland Browns stadium stood there, so I had a very limited view of the water. In the distance, a dinky sailboat was too far away to see and appreciate. I thought God surely must have a warped sense of humor if he thought this was a nice view.

"It sure is an ugly view, isn't it?"

It was not the Lord speaking this time, not unless His voice had changed from that morning. It was the man standing next to me. I looked over and he was still staring out over the water. I acknowledged his opinion by agreeing. He stood up straight and smiled at me, saying, "You know, I don't even know why I'm here." I told him that I was not sure why I was there either.

Then he walked toward me and stuck out his hand. "Hi, my name is John. What's yours?"

Chapter 9

I could only suppose that this was him—the man the Lord had told me about—but in my mind he did not look anything like I thought he would. I was confronted with a man named John, just like I had been told. Could God be pointing me to this person? Perhaps I had better make sure before I made any hasty conclusions. I asked John what his last name was. I asked John what his last name was and he replied "My friends call me Just John."

Bingo! God's Spirit began to flood over me. It was not long before I felt as if my feet were about five inches off the ground. Of course, John had no idea what thoughts were going on inside of me. I had to know where this John came from and what kind of person he was.

John told me he had just come back from California where he lived for the past fifteen years.

He had gotten into trouble there and had spent some time in jail. The state of California had granted him parole very shortly before he came back to his home state and hometown. He intended to start a new life. He spoke freely to me, as though he had known me a long time. His openness made me feel that I should tell him why I was there and what my thoughts were about the possible connection between him and me. It seemed to take me forever to get the words out because I was so excited and nervous. Finally, I was able to tell him that I had a spiritual reason for being at the park that day.

He was quiet for a few moments and looked at me with a strange expression. Then he told me that he had felt as though he had been led to the park that day too, not knowing why and having no reason to explain it. Then I asked the question.

"Just John," I addressed him, "Do you know the Lord?"

He smiled and told me that if I was asking him if he was a Christian or not, the answer was yes. He added, "I would have to say that the Lord and I are pretty good friends." That answer was good enough for me. I knew that this was the man I was supposed to meet.

John asked, "Why did you ask that question?"

I told him that he would think I was completely crazy if I told him, but God had opened the door for me to tell him, so I would.

"I'm on a spiritual mission, and I'm not sure what it's all about," I said. "I know that I am supposed to meet someone named John today, and that he is supposed to help me build a church. I prayed about it this morning and asked God what the name of this man would be, and He told me, 'Just John.'" I continued telling him about my message, and John listened closely to every word. He looked almost stunned as I told him. "He said that my birthday, halfway houses, and prison ministries would play a major role."

John's eyes looked larger and more intense when I told him this. After all, he had just mentioned prison in his story about his own life. Then he asked me, "What is your birthday?"

"June 26, 1951."

"You aren't serious, are you? I can't believe it," said John.

I felt challenged, as if he had some reason to doubt me. "Huh? Of course, it is," I said as I dug through my purse to retrieve my license. With great surprise, John began to chuckle.

"What about you?" I said. "Where is your license?"

He pulled out his wallet and handed me his license. I couldn't believe my eyes. He truly was born on the same day and year as I was. Wow! I was kind of breathless when I said, "John, I think maybe the John that I'm looking for is you."

We talked awhile, but then I had to leave for my appointment at the May Company. He and I made plans to meet later in the day around 6:00 p.m. in front of the May Company building. Deep down, I knew that this was the man I was supposed to find, and I naturally wanted to know more about him. Six o'clock could not come fast enough. I was incredibly eager to talk with him. The Lord was bringing things together quickly after a long and uncertain wait and many, many prayers.

Chapter 10

$\mathcal{M}$y meeting at the May Company turned out successfully, just like the others on this special trip for my new area. God was still giving to me in a big way. His biggest gift, I felt, was yet to come—that is, if John showed up.

At 6:00 p.m. sharp, I was out in front of the May Company. There was no way I was going to miss meeting up with John. I had to assure myself that this was the right John for my mission. Fifteen minutes later, there was still no John. I was nervous. Five minutes later, he was still not there. I decided to wait only a half hour because the stores were closing and this was a bad area; the street people were becoming visible. I thought back to Dorothy's admonition earlier in the day and knew that I should heed it, if it was necessary.

Luckily it was not. In a short while, John came down the street, walking and smiling widely. He told me that he was surprised to see me because he did not think I would show up, but his curiosity finally overcame him and he strolled downtown to see if I was there. We found an Italian restaurant that was open near the downtown area so we went there to have supper and continue our conversation.

We talked for hours. Getting to know each other was easy. John was comfortable with conversation and our ideas just flowed back and forth. Maybe it was not good to feel this way, but I was attracted to him, because he made me feel like I was a real person with intelligence, confidence, and self-esteem. It had been a long time since someone had made me feel like John did that evening. Yes, the Lord did heal me and lift me up when I was saved and He did set me on the right track, but there is nothing like being affirmed and accepted by another human to reinforce positive feelings and to give a person more interest in life.

That night, John tapped in to the beauty that the Lord had built within me. I felt refreshed by our time together. It was almost as if we had known each other all of our lives. Talking to each other came easily, even though that first glance earlier in the day gave me the impression that this man was not for me. Maybe he was rough on the outside, but inside, he was a jewel. John encouraged me to pursue the path the Lord had laid before me. He instilled confidence in me by the way he talked, even though I could tell he lacked confidence in himself in some area of his life.

John told me he was willing to help me in my quest to build a church in any way he could, even though there was no way that he thought he could be the John that I was supposed to find. Later on, in our relationship, I learned that John came from a very poor home life that had deeply affected the way he had lived his life and the way he still lived it. As a child, John was beaten and verbally abused by his father. This abuse ruined John's self-esteem, and it sent a demon that he wrestled with throughout his life. Because John's self-esteem was low, he always thought of himself as not capable enough, not good-looking enough, and unable to have stability in his life. Even in his insecurity and self-deprecating attitude, John was able to make others feel secure. He knew how to build up confidence in others and make them feel worthwhile. This was a gift God had given him.

Our first night together, I learned that John was staying in a halfway house in downtown Cleveland as a part of his parole from the State of California. John had served time for robbery before he was paroled in a slightly unusual procedure. He was allowed to come back to Ohio, although most parolees were required to stay in the state of their conviction. He had been released a month later than he should have been. As we thought about his late release and his being in Cleveland, both John and I thought it was probably God's perfect timing so that John could be where he needed to be on the day I was seeking to find him.

After spending several hours at the restaurant, we agreed to write to each other. Sadly, I had to go back to Pennsylvania. When we parted that first time, I felt as if I was leaving a long-lost friend. We met on October 24, 1984. We were both thirty-three years old. John reminded me that this was the age of Jesus when He died on the cross. I could see that God's plan was working, and it was unfolding right then, right before my eyes.

Chapter 11

The days and weeks after meeting John were more interesting than they had been in the past. My faith had not always been strong, but with the introduction of John into the picture, it took on a whole new luster. It seemed to me that the words the Lord said to me now had a much deeper meaning. I felt closer to accomplishing the jobs He had for me than I ever had before. The helpmate that God promised me long ago was now known to me, and I was sure we would be blessed as long as we continued to seek and do His will.

One of the earliest manifestations of God's blessings came during the period between my leaving John on that October day and the day before Christmas Eve. If I wanted to talk to John, all I had to do was ask the Lord where he would be at such-and-such time, and I was always led to him. The bond between us was electrifying, and I believe it was all the Lord's doings. He was bonding us together in a strong way so that we could build His church.

Our spiritual connection was beyond amazing. I always told John that he was my mirror image. My strengths were his weaknesses, and my weaknesses were his strengths. It was as if we could sense what was going on inside of each other. When something was not right, even across many miles, we both seemed to sense it and took time to talk about it and help the other to straighten out the problem. There is no question in my mind that this was all happening through God, and God used us greatly in this way to teach us, chastise us, and sensitize us.

As an example, about a month after I met John, I was praying one evening and I felt the Lord tell me that He was going to let me experience all of John's emotions for three days. I know this may sound a bit cosmic, but it is typical of the way the Lord worked with us and through us. I know it is different for everyone, but this was His way with us. Although I did not understand this whole experience at the time, I later realized that I had become a judgmental and condemning person in my life, and God wanted to root that out of me. He did. God wanted me to see things from another perspective—His.

Those three days were a total living hell for me. The emotions I felt were horrifying and foreign to me in their depth. I sensed great fear, anger, emptiness, sorrow, and lack of purpose during those three days. It was very hard for me to separate my feelings from John's, and all of these emotions just wore me down mentally. It seemed that the waves of emotions never seemed to stop, and it gave me a whole new appreciation of John as a person. His feelings and thoughts were just as intense, if not more so, than mine.

At the end of the third day, John called me, and I practically burst trying to share my experience with him. "John, I have to tell you something. Three days ago, the Lord allowed me to experience your emotions along with my own. I know it sounds odd, and believe me, it was. On the first morning, I woke up early with an emotional civil war going on in my head. Prior to this emotional upheaval, I felt the Lord ask me if I would willingly share your feelings so I could understand you better, and I agreed. Were you fighting or arguing with someone around eight o'clock in the morning three days ago?"

"Yes, I was," John replied. "I had a run-in with the guy that manages the halfway house where I am staying and I got angry. He didn't want to give me a pass to leave, and all I could think of was not being able to call you at noon the way we had planned it last week. I was furious."

As we dove into our emotions deeper, I realized the feelings I was experiencing were right on the money. "John, I could hardly carry the weight of emotion I felt the entire first day. It was full of pain, sorrow, guilt, restlessness, and anguish. I'm not sure if there was any emotion I didn't experience both physically and mentally. The second day of this emotional rollercoaster ride was not as wild. The second day, I felt extreme emptiness and sadness, as if you were feeling unwanted and rejected. Could that be true?"

His voice was full of sadness as he said he had gotten together with his father that afternoon to ask forgiveness for the mess he made out of his life. "My dad was still very angry with me for making such a mess of things with our family. When he left that day, I wasn't sure he would ever speak to me again. Just seeing my dad gave me joy, yet the rejection and emptiness I was left with were excruciating."

"I was frightened for you, John," I said. "The third day was a stormy day for you, wasn't it? You were thinking you made a big mistake coming back to Ohio. I could feel hate, despair, great sadness, and thoughts of suicide. Is that correct?"

John said nothing. Several moments went by before he said anything. "If it wasn't for you, I probably wouldn't be here today," he said.

I was grateful when John's emotions were no longer present within me. It was such a heavy weight to carry around. We discussed the events of those three days for quite a while. *Unusual* and *eerie* were just a few words to describe my experience that weekend. It taught me to respect and not judge what other people think or how they behave. The Lord was not done with me yet. The experience cured me of being judgmental. It was a tough but invaluable growing experience for me to share John's feelings. I learned that we all struggle, we are all different, and we are all God's children. If He loves me as I know He does and loves John in the same way, then who am I to put him down for the way he looks or expresses himself? God is the one true judge. We are not. We should never pass judgment on one person or another, because, being imperfect ourselves, we always pass an imperfect judgment on others.

Before I met John, and if the Lord had not led me to him, I would not have given John the proverbial "time of day." I would have been afraid to be around him because of his background and the way he looked. His background and lifestyle dictated how he appeared when I met him. The years had not been kind to John; in turn, John had not been kind to the years either. God was helping John to overcome his problems. My being judgmental and stubborn toward John was counteracting the good work that God was trying to do.

When the Lord brought us together, John had been divorced for fifteen years and had two daughters who would have nothing to do with him. John lived with great heartache because of the bridges he had burned in the past. He also carried around many other deep scars that would surface now and then. Early in his childhood, there had been abuse by his father, and over the years, the severe drug use had taken a toll on him as well. The empathy that I was able to feel in experiencing John's feelings was a way for the Lord to show me how to treat others.

How does God do this in your life? He does it, you know. In my case, He let me understand the feelings of another person, one I previously would have turned away from and shunned. By experiencing those three days of terrible feelings of inadequacy and sadness, I learned to be understanding. The Lord bonded us.

God teaches us how to better serve His people and grow in the power of the faith. After a year of long-distance dating and calling, writing, and driving back and forth to see each other, John and I finally got together when I decided to move closer to the Cleveland area. The job with Oceans West gradually fizzled after the investors and owners turned away from the shoe line before it had a chance to succeed. Worse yet for me, the company owed me money and could not or would not pay. I had to find another job to pay the bills for my family and me. I decided that this loss of a job and money was just another test for me of my faith.

I looked for a job in Ohio and found one with PCA Photography Studios at the May Company. I had my training at Trautman's Department store in Greensburg, Pennsylvania, where I used to work years earlier. PCA Photography had a studio there. It was comforting to train in my old stomping grounds. The job was given to me with only a month left before school let out for the summer, so my mother stayed home with Tina and Geoff while I moved to Ohio and prepared to make the biggest change in my life and the lives of my children.

The structure of my family and my life was about to change in a very big way. Unlike many other long-distance romances, this one between John and me grew stronger while we were apart because we were watched over by the man upstairs. We guarded our hearts for each other, prayed for each other, and shared everything we possibly could. John and I avoided trouble together and found our joy together. We found our joy in thanking God often for bringing us together to do His work in the world. But at that point, I really wasn't sure exactly where, when, or how that would take place.

Chapter 12

When I decided to move to Ohio, I had no idea where I was going to live and had no money to find a place. Any money I had would have to go toward the bills that had accumulated. Not being paid by my former company had put me in a sad situation. Even though the Lord was unfolding a plan, there were still many areas of my life that held uncertainty and unresolved problems. I trusted in God and forged ahead because I believed He wanted me to get busy for His purpose.

Two problems still loomed before me: the sale of my house and the finalizing of the divorce terms. I needed a buyer for the house, but somehow I knew that this would happen. I had made the decision that if I was going to go to Ohio, the Lord would make it possible for John and me to be together to follow the Lord's guidance.

Months before I moved, John had been released from the halfway house in downtown Cleveland. He had a little money and found a small apartment in Lakewood, and all indications were that he and I would live together. On one of my trips to Ohio, sometime in late November of 1984, the Lord impressed upon me that I was to pick up John and go to a Methodist church somewhere that evening. The impression became stronger as I prayed and continued on toward Cleveland.

I drove by a church that I felt was the one to which we were to go. As I drove closer to it, I saw that it was a Methodist church. I picked up John and we went to that Methodist church at 7:00p.m.— the time that the Lord told me to go. On the way, I explained to John what we were supposed to go there, and he willingly accepted my explanation. We were supposed to go to the church and—as one— dedicate ourselves to each other and to God. We were also supposed to promise Him that we would do His will for our lives.

The dedication of John and me to God and to each other was supposed to be witnessed by Michael the Archangel. Even though I know this whole situation sounds very odd, John had no qualms about our plans for dedication. He was more than willing and ready to take this big step.

Michael is God's greatest warring angel, and the glow from his presence is impossible to describe. In Revelations 12:7–10, he is sent to hold back evil so that God's people prevail against darkness. I think that if Michael was to be a witness to our dedication to God and each other, it said a lot about God's plans for our lives. As we would learn later, we surely needed help holding back the evil that would come against us. I found the church that I had passed earlier in the day, and we drove into the back parking lot. As we walked toward the church, we saw a light and the back door was open.

We walked in just as the minister was walking out. He saw us, stopped, and asked, "Can I help you?" John and I looked at each other, smiled, and without a word walked over to the pastor to explain our intent.

John said, "Nora and I came here to pray. We have never been here before, so we aren't quite sure where the sanctuary is. Could you show us?"

"We know it's unusual for us to come here this evening," I added, "but in my prayers today I believed that the Lord wanted us to be here this evening at seven o'clock to pray and dedicate our lives to Him and to each other."

The pastor looked puzzled. After a few seconds of taking it all in he said, "That's funny, because usually the church isn't open Thursday evenings. The choir decided at the last minute to throw in an extra rehearsal for the Christmas pageant. Please, allow me." He motioned toward the sanctuary and walked us to the entrance. "When you are done, please leave quietly and close the doors to the sanctuary," he said. He told us to have a good evening, then made his way back to the church office.

We ventured down the main aisle and chose a place to sit. Was it a coincidence? I think not. There was no doubt that we were exactly where we were supposed to be. In our minds, we knew that God had made all of the necessary arrangements for us that evening.

The sanctuary felt cozy and comfortable. We stood there admiring the intricate details carved all around us. We walked about halfway down the aisle and started to move into a section of seats to the right. The church was unique in that there were no pews, just movie theater-style seats. I started to tell

John more about how St. Michael the Archangel was there somewhere to witness our commitment.

Finding some seats about halfway to the altar, John moved in ahead of me. Just as he started to sit down, the seat between us came down very heavily—*whoosh*—as if someone very large had just flopped down on it. We were both taken by surprise and just stared at the seat, knowing we had not touched it ourselves. Trying to lighten up the mood, John said as he pointed to the seat, "All I know is if he picks up his seat, I'm out of here."

We then moved down an extra seat so we would not disturb our "guest." Could it possibly be St. Michael? We began praying, knowing full well that it was God's blessing for us to be in this place. The Lord led us in our prayers as we dedicated our lives to His service. Oh, let's not forget our witness to this dedication, Michael the Archangel himself. How enchanted that evening felt. When John and I parted that night, I truly felt as if he and I were married, even though the legal customs of the world had not been followed. God had brought us together and now, it seemed, He had bound us together. It would be forever. It would be no other way.

For me, it was interesting that the Lord had tied me to an ex-convict and I felt comfortable about it. A year before, I never would have imagined it or accepted it because of what people around me would have thought and said, and because of my own biases. God had changed me, and I was a different person with different ideas. The outward things did not matter as much to me anymore. Now it was the Spirit that guided me.

On the way back to my home in West Newton, Pennsylvania, I found myself on the Ohio turnpike following a station wagon all the way from Cleveland to exit seven on the Pennsylvania turnpike. Normally when driving, I did not have much patience following another car, but that night, I did. It would bring about another example of God watching over me. The station wagon in front of me had a dark-complected, dark-haired driver who sat tall in the seat. I observed that he must be a very tall man, because when he reached to get his ticket at the toll booth, his arm was exceedingly long with a heavy gold bracelet on his wrist. His skin had a copper glow to it.

I felt that this man in front of me was St. Michael, there to assure me a safe ride home. Though he might not have liked it, the driver was probably aware that I was closely following behind His station wagon. In my mind, I visualized a tow-bar connecting my car to his. That impression stayed very strong and made me feel safe during the entire three and a half hours of my trip. I felt I was being protected by God's greatest warrior.

All along the highway that night, police were pulling over car after car, as if there was something unusual going on. However, neither the station wagon driver nor I was ever stopped. Again, I felt protected by some force that I knew was there but could not see or understand. Maybe it is better sometimes to accept by faith what we do not understand rather than to try to find rational explanations for everything. I believe that our lives are full of situations that we can accept as coincidental or attribute to a greater unknown force guiding us in the right direction.

Chapter 13

*B*y May of 1985, my training with PCA Photo Studios was complete. I started my position as a studio portrait sales manager at what was then called the May Company in Parmatown Mall in Parma, Ohio. John and I moved into a one-room efficiency apartment that he had been renting in Lakewood. By the time Tina and Geoff were out of school, I had sold my house. A former babysitter for my children who was still one of my friends had told me repeatedly how much she loved my house and that if I ever wanted to sell it, she wanted to know. Well, sure enough, she took me up on my offer and legally assumed the mortgage.

I took Tina and Geoff back to Ohio and temporarily we all stayed in very cramped quarters. After only four weeks, I found a farm house in Olmsted Falls that had much character and historical elegance.

This home had three bedrooms upstairs, one downstairs, an office, a huge living room, a kitchen, and even a dining room. The old white farm home had a huge old-fashioned front porch. The backyard was fairly large with a big weeping willow tree in the corner and a newly constructed barn-shaped shed at the rear.

It was a lovely place to live, and the town was very quaint. The houses and buildings were old, yet well kept. In the fall, the children went to one of the best schools in the area and they made new friends and did well in school. We all felt very happy.

John began working with a restoration company doing repairs, remodeling, and painting of older homes and buildings. We joined Olmsted Falls Christian Church, and life was a definite improvement. John and I started planning our wedding and set a date for February 15, 1986. I consented to living together until the wedding date. I convinced myself it was okay. As much as it seemed we were all supposed to be together, surely this wouldn't make a difference in God's plan. After all, we already dedicated our lives to Him and each other.

Now as I look back on this decision, I see things differently. Finding a church was so important to us.

After searching, we found a church in North Olmsted and started attending right away. I didn't want to live life without the Lord in it. Plus, it was very important to me to give stability and structure to my children's lives. We all enjoyed attending church each week, and before you knew it, John and I were teaching children's Bible study after our church service. We loved the people there and it was easy to volunteer to do things anytime the church had something going on.

Time moved swiftly then, and for a while, my focus was the wedding and not my relationship with the Lord. Although I prayed and spent time with Him daily, I know deep in my heart I was not happy with my decision to live with John before marriage and it kept me from feeling the closeness with both John and the Lord that I had felt in the past. My decision haunted me.

Chapter 14

*W*e were married in February at Olmsted Christian Church with about forty guests present. Our small reception was held at the home of my friends Pam and Greg. Despite the inner nagging in my heart, things were moving along. Time was passing quickly and life seemed enjoyable for all of us. Being married to John was the completion of faith and commitment we had made earlier in our relationship to each other and to the Lord.

Our spare time was often spent with Pam and Greg and their children, Missy and Josh, whose ages were close to that of my own children. We played games like Uno, Scrabble, and different card games for hours at a time. Pam and Greg's landlords, Elie and Jim, lived upstairs and used to come downstairs to share in our fun. Elie and my John were always battling each other's wits playing Scrabble. When he came home from prison to Ohio, Elie and Jim took John under their wing. They were like parents to us and loved John very much.

Elie belonged to a prison ministry and had (at the request of John's brother-in-law) written to John while he was still in jail. Elie was a godsend when John needed friends the most. John and I felt blessed to have such loving friends; we were like one big, happy family. We got together regularly to share each other's company as well as to give support in times of need. Pam and I were best of friends, and John and Greg became good friends as well. We went on picnics together, went swimming and shopping, and attended special events as a group.

Does it sound like the perfect life? Well, it could have been. There were changes that started to become evident with my husband. I knew he must have started using marijuana again and was obviously drinking.

He began to come home later from work at night and always seemed to have an attitude toward me. If John drank, then I became his reason, his excuse. His own guilt created a monster. At first, the changes were subtle. For example, he would verbally threaten to hurt me, and as time went on, the words were not enough. He began to push me. Then he became more violent, slamming me against the wall and grabbing me by the throat while he called me horrible names. After a while, I became scared. How far would John go to carry out his threats? The more he drank, the worse he became. This became a serious problem not long after we were married. It was hard to imagine that this was the same person I had met that day in the park and had married with so much faith in the future.

Next, John lost his job, having some sort of unbelievable excuse. A recurring thought in my mind was, *What have I done to cause this? How could this be happening? How could I have let this happen in my life?* Perhaps I had not had enough faith in John. Was I a bad person who created this monster? I was devastated. There I was again, starting to think that I was this horrible person who was doomed to have a terrible life, but now I had dragged my children into it.

I remember onetime, John and I had a big fight, resulting in threats and accusations. He even ripped the phone out of the wall and wrapped the cord around my neck and tried to choke me. I survived, but barely. The following morning after John had left the house, I went into my bedroom and fell to my knees. I threw myself flat down on the floor with my face against the carpet. I sobbed for hours, asking God the same question over and over: *why?* I knew that I had made a commitment to God that I could not break, but how could I go on this way?

I asked God to forgive me, for I felt so much anger and bitterness toward John. If I could not get out of this marriage, what was the answer? I believed my marital vows, "Till death do us part." My mind could not take much more. Maybe John would die, or maybe I would be the one.

How could I even think such thoughts? God, forgive me, please. I was so sorry for my thoughts. I finally found enough strength to crawl into bed and fell into a deep sleep. The next thing I knew I was sitting bolt upright in bed. Sweat was pouring off me, and I was screaming and sobbing out loud. I'd had a horrible dream.

I was standing in front of the old church that I went to as a child. It was a symbol of something. What was it? In my dream, I opened the doors and walked into the foyer and stood while I looked around, absorbing the surroundings. Could it be? Somehow, it was supposed to represent John. It was

John, yet it was the inside of a church. There were large white pillars that supported the structure.

Up on the altar was a beautiful golden chalice filled with a white sparkling powdered substance. It had a glow about it and a power pulled me close to it. There was a great desire to touch it, to taste it. As I started to move toward the front of the church, the ground around me and under me started to tremble. Somehow, I knew that the structure was going to collapse. If John was to live, I had to get the chalice out before the building tumbled to the ground. Could I do this? I had to. A voice told me in the dream, *Go. Get it now before it's too late. John will die if you don't.*

I somehow was able to get the chalice outside only seconds before the building went crumbling to the ground. The church was attended. Some of the powder had spilled out of the chalice in the process, but somehow, I knew that it would replenish itself. As I held it in my hands, I knew it was all that was left of John. Yet I knew the glowing substance would overflow once more.

I wished John would die. I prayed God would forgive me. I cried and asked forgiveness again for all of my terrible feelings. After this spiritual dream or experience, I continued to seek guidance for months from God about the continuing problems I was facing. As if in answer to my prayers, John finally quit smoking dope and drinking heavily. Sometimes he would stay completely sober or just dabbled very lightly in a drink or two. Things seemed to be looking up once more.

Chapter 15

*O*nce John had gotten a grip on his life again and had started going to church, life became bearable once more. The difference in John was heartwarming. Watching him get involved with Sunday school at church reinforced my feelings that he was a good man.

He had a soft spot for children, mainly because of his inability to be with his own. He grew to love Tina and Geoff very much, and on many occasions told me how thankful he was to have them as a part of his life. True, it was sad that he had no contact with his own daughters, but it never stopped him from loving them, thinking about them, or praying for them. I knew if I ever was able to meet them, I would hope to be able to tell them good things about their father. Maybe someday Kimberly Ann and Rachael Gail Dawn will somehow know their father.

I thanked God for whom John had become. What a change he had made! Another change that John made was in jobs. He became a warehouse manager for a design company. Along with the new job came a new house for all of us to live in. We were not able to buy one yet, but we moved to Middleburg Heights, where Tina and Geoff switched to a new school system—one that was ranked even higher than the last one they attended. This made us feel better about the move and the new situation.

We loved farmhouses, so we found another one where we rented the downstairs half, which was a few less rooms then the house in Olmsted Falls but still plenty big for all of us. We had the use of the front yard, and the front door was ours. The yard was surrounded by large pine trees that kept out the noise of the busy street in front. Also, in the center of the yard was a beautiful old cherry tree. The whole scene was pleasant to us and we felt very much at home.

Besides settling into this comfortable old farmhouse, John loved his job, and I was able to get a new job with Revelations Shoes at a retail store in Parmatown Mall as the store manager. It seemed as if all was going well and we could begin to think ahead. We hoped to start saving money to purchase a new house of our own in a year or so. God was shining on us, and there was hope, love, and happiness once more.

Sometimes, when things are going smoothly and you hit a snag, you wonder why. In some situations, we never seem to understand why things happen as they do. Later, it becomes clearer. The day after Thanksgiving, something did happen.

John took me to work at the mall since he did not have to work that day. Tina and Geoff didn't have school that day, so they all went to Pam and Greg's home for the day. When I walked into the store, before I started my paperwork, I took out my Bible. I started to read for about a half hour. I felt something was very wrong that day, but I couldn't imagine what it was.

During the day, a man whose wife had bought shoes from me the week before stopped in to see how I was. The gentleman, his wife, and I were sharing our feelings about our belief in Jesus as the Son of God the week before. It turned out that the man was a minister and, on the side, worked at the music shop that was up the hall from my store in the mall. During my visit with him, he shared a story about his sister who had been married three times. Her first husband died of cancer, and that was a terrible ordeal for her. Her second husband was an alcoholic who abused her. She divorced him and eventually married again, only to have her third husband die of an aneurysm.

As he told me about his sister's life, I empathized with the woman, even though I didn't know her. I asked the man how she was coping with all of this, and he told me that each time she faced a tragedy in her life, she would hear a voice say to her, *This, too, shall pass.* Somehow, I felt this preacher was trying to give me a message.

All day long, these words kept ringing in my ear. *This, too, shall pass.* I tried everything to brush off the fear I had that something bad was going to happen— something that needed some strong spiritual help. I prayed as much as possible that day. According to Psalm 91 (KJV), "He will give His angels charge concerning you, to guard you in all your ways." I tried to hold on to that Scripture as much as I could. When I opened my crystal-etched box filled with Scripture passages, it was this verse I pulled out: "Trust in the Lord with all thine heart; and lean not unto thine own understanding. In all thy ways acknowledge

Him and He shall direct thy paths" (Proverbs 3:5–6 KJV).

Somehow, reading this particular verse did not help me relax very much; in the past, it seemed that every time I pulled out that Scripture, I ended up facing one of the big trials of my life. Finally, my workday ended, and I proceeded to the mall parking lot to wait for John's arrival. John's being late and the anticipation of his arrival created more fears. The only time he was ever late was when he had been drinking. Was this the case tonight? "God, protect me from harm's way. In Jesus's name, I pray."

It was nearly an hour before John arrived. My heart was in my stomach. Was the past returning? As the car came closer to where I was waiting, I could see John's face. It was there—that evil look he always got when he was full of guilt. My concern for Geoff's safety unnerved me. He was only twelve years old, and I was afraid for him because of John's driving. Geoff was in the backseat and he did not look happy. The knot in my stomach began to grow. The pain became more nauseating.

As we drove onto the main street, John's driving was horrendous. John immediately began to blame me for his tardiness. He became more and more upset with me because he could see I was afraid of his driving and his behavior. John grabbed me by the arm, tugging at me and yelling at me, wanting to know what my problem was. Finally, I told him that he was scaring me with his driving, and he became enraged. The yelling and screaming began to get worse. Finally, he pulled over and insisted that I drive. This was something he usually did if he knew he had had too much to drink. I could not understand why he hadn't done this before now. Perhaps at this point in our relationship, he knew that the use of excessive alcohol was not tolerable to me.

He stopped the car and I moved from the passenger side to the driver's side. As I did so, John walked toward the curb as if he would get into the passenger side of the car. Then he stopped. He looked up at me and insisted that I drive home without him. "If you think your driving is better than mine, then you drive home without me. Do it. I don't need you, you pathetic creature." John screamed continuous profanity at me and physical threats. I took off, leaving him behind.

Was it wrong? It would be a long walk home for him. It was very cold that night and he didn't have a heavy coat on. My God, what should I do? If the walk does not sober him up, then he will be even more furious with me. My thoughts ran wild. I was scared. Not having a phone installed at the house yet, I would not be able to call for help if I needed to do so.

After we arrived home, I gave Geoff a quarter. "Keep this in your room. If John gets crazy, I'll send you for help. You can use the pay phone down the street at Dairy Mart." I sent Geoff to his room and asked God to protect him and me from harm's way. *This, too, shall pass* came crashing back in my mind. Over and over in my head, I could hear these words. Also, the Scripture from Psalm 91:11 came back to me: "He will give His angels charge concerning you, to guard you in all your ways."

I was never as scared in all my life as I was right then, waiting for John to come home. I paced back and forth. Finally, I heard John coming up the driveway. The door opened and a madman came crashing in. John came right at me, grabbing me by the arm, screaming things at me that made no sense at all, calling me by the name of a man who had raped me when I was younger, saying, "It's you, I know it is. Admit it. Say your name, you disgusting coward. I'm going to kill you for what you did to her."

John kept pushing me, telling me to say this man's name. I tried calling to John, telling him it was me, Nora, but the more I said my name, the more determined he became that I was lying to him. I pleaded with him. "John, stop it, please! It's Nora!" By now I had been backhanded across the face over and over again. My clothes were torn from John's pulling and dragging as he continued his attack. Blow after blow landed me against the furniture in the living room as well as against the walls. Never stopping the verbal obscenities, he continued his threats to hurt me.

Who was this man? No matter how much I tried to get John back to reality, I couldn't. I tried getting away from him and could not. By now, I was in great pain. My face was obviously swollen. When I tried to talk, my lips could not form the words. My brain was numb with confusion. John dragged me down the hall to the doorway of our bedroom. I tried once more to get away, but he knocked me to the ground. I went unconscious for a few minutes. I could hear John as I started to come to, saying that if I didn't get up, he would kill me. Then he grabbed me by the neck and started choking me. I had no energy to stop him. I felt as if there was no use trying to stop him anymore. He was a raving maniac, and I could not stop him.

It was at that moment when I seemed to feel something coming between my neck and John's hands. It was like a pair of invisible hands to guard me from any further pressure. Somehow, in my semiconscious state, I felt protected. Something was fighting my battle for me. John picked me up by the arms and started dragging me toward the kitchen, telling me to fight like a man and stand on my own two feet. While we were still in the hall, I managed to yell for Geoff to get out of the house and run. Just as he started out to leave his bedroom, John said if Geoff tried to leave, he would kill him, too. Of course, I had no choice but to send Geoff back to his room. I was grateful Tina was spending the night at her girlfriend's. She was not as emotionally strong as Geoff was at the time. This would have traumatized her.

John again began to drag me toward the kitchen saying he was going to slit my throat. He was still talking to me like I was someone else. He turned on the kitchen light to search for a knife and then saw my face for the first time. Instantly, his facial expression changed. The evil was now gone. All I could see was confusion and hurt. My real husband was back, full of sorrow, realizing what he must have done to me. John was lost for words. All he could do was apologize to me, saying, "Please forgive me, Nora."

He wanted me to go lie down by him in bed. All I wanted was to get my son and run away, but, not knowing if the demon in John would return or not, I went into the bedroom and lay down beside him. My body was trembling all over and I could not stop crying. I was in shock. John was crying and repeatedly mumbling, "Don't leave me." My mind was screaming with thoughts of pain all over my body and the desire to get up and leave, to get out of this terrible ordeal. I could barely move from all the blows I had suffered; my chest hurt, and, because of my injured throat, I could hardly breathe. I thought for sure that I was dying.

After about an hour, John passed out. I was terrified and in great pain, but I slowly crawled out of bed, made my way to Geoff's door, and carefully went in for him. To my disbelief, he was dressed and ready to leave the house. Geoff didn't say anything. He responded to my motions and I directed him to get his stuff and leave. I know he was afraid and confused. Just knowing what he witnessed broke my heart.

Quietly, we made our way out of the house and to the car. I started the car and drove off with Geoff before John had a chance to catch us. At last we were safe, but I did not know what to do or where to go. I just knew we had to get away. My thoughts ran rampant through my mind. What have I done to my son? Devastation came over me. I could not believe what a horrific nightmare I had just experienced, but more importantly, what had I just put Geoff through? How tragic this was for him. Heaviness gripped me as I thought of my twelve-year-old son having to work through this the rest of his life.

Chapter 16

As I drove Geoff and myself away from the house, I had no idea where I was going to go. I was crying and trying to drive sensibly, and I asked God to tell me where to go. From somewhere came the answer: I would go to my friend's house in North Olmsted, somewhere that John would never in a million years think to look. Sometime later, still hurting, yet trying to be calm, I pulled into their driveway in the middle of the night. I told Geoff to wait in the car, and I knocked on the door hoping they would hear me. Finally, the porch light came on and a man peeked out from behind the curtains of the side door to see who was brash enough to knock at that hour of the night. It was Chuck. I could tell he was not sure at first who I was.

"Chuck, it's me, Nora. I need help."

Without further delay, he opened the door. "My God, what happened to you? Are you all right? Where are the kids?"

I motioned for Geoff to get out of the car and tried to explain what had happened as Chuck hustled Geoff and me inside. Fran came downstairs to our rescue as well. I told them what had happened, although it was probably not completely clear because I was only filling in some of the detail. As we discussed the whole situation, I explained that my daughter, Tina, had not been there during this ordeal. She had decided early in the day to spend the night at her girlfriend's house. They agreed that this was a blessing since they and I knew that Tina was not as emotionally strong as Geoff was. She might never have survived that night of violence. I thanked God for her not being around to witness any of it.

Chuck and Fran looked at my injuries carefully and insisted I go to the hospital to be checked out. Fran stayed at the house to attend to Geoff, getting him settled in. Very reluctantly, I went to the hospital with Chuck. When the name of the hospital appeared before me, I was repulsed. It was St. John West Shore Hospital, and at this time, I wanted nothing to do with anything named John. However,

I knew that Chuck would not let me leave without being checked over.

It was humiliating for me to be in this situation, being stared at—or so I thought—by the emergency room visitors and personnel. I could not face anyone. To make it less difficult for me, the nurses let me sit in a separate waiting room. I was still crying and shaking; it was a nightmare, but I was awake. How could this have happened! It seemed like forever that I sat there with a damp cloth on my face while I continued to saturate it with tears. Again, there came to me the words, *This, too, shall pass.* This passage rang over and over in my head as I sat there thinking that nothing could be worse than this.

The emergency room doctor on duty that night was an Indian woman who was very sympathetic to my situation. She felt that I should press charges that night, but I couldn't bring myself to do it for fear that if the charges resulted in a conviction, when John was released from jail, he would come back to kill me for sure. The good news she had for me was that I would live. The X-rays showed nothing broken; however, my voice box had been badly damaged. The extent of the injuries could not be determined because of the swelling. The doctor said it would be at least two or three weeks before it could be looked at closely. She also said it would be at least that long before the true color of my face and half of my body would start to look normal. Many of the bruises were already becoming very visible.

Did she say I would live? Lucky me. That was easy for her to say. As for me, I felt dead inside. I remember thinking that there was no way that I could get through all of this. It was going to take a miracle to get past this experience. This was by far the worst day of my life.

Emotionally I was depleted. Physically I was broken. My pulse pounded through my body like a steel drum being played over and over. I knew I asked for God's help, but I'm not sure what I said. There was so much sorrow, hurt, guilt, and pain running rampant through my body that I couldn't think straight.

Chapter 17

I do believe in miracles. Over the next couple of months, John and I spoke often. I gave him a list of requirements that would have to be met before he would be given a chance to come home. We met with Pastor Doug weekly at Southwest Christian Church where we had been attending since our move to Middleburg Heights. Pastor Doug counseled us through the rules that would need to be followed as well as the emotional healing that needed to take place. Tina and Geoff eventually sat in on some of the sessions so that they could better understand what happened and what to do next.

With deep thought and much prayer, John was given what would be his last chance to redeem himself and approval to come home. Somehow it seemed that the most important part of our relationship was that God had brought us together for His purpose. It was up to us to try to achieve this, however we could.

Most of our lives, we go from day to day trying to achieve whatever goals we have set for ourselves. Whether at our job, at school, or in a relationship, once in a while we take a chance. Depending on how you look at things, it could be called stepping out in faith—faith in what you cannot see. That was where John and I were. We had to trust in each other and believe in what we could not see in our future.

I must say that for quite some time after this tragic time in our lives, our lives began to improve once more. We were attending church more often. Our jobs were going well, and everything around us had a different and uplifting light about it. One of the prophecies that God had given me was about Revelations. Of course, I thought he meant the end times. What it came to be was that for the next seven years, I would work at a shoe store called Revelations. The prophecy I had been given years earlier said that Revelations would play a big part in my life. Could there be a connection to the store?

Another prophecy that God provided to me for my faith was that He would give back to me what I left behind (my friends, family, and a home) by following Him. This would be a gift to me, because I left everything when I moved to Ohio that gave me a sense of security, love, and support.

In the spring of 1988, on my way home from work, I started to think about all of the wonderful things that had become a part of my life. I had a new family, but I still had my own family. Although no one can take the place of your own father, John's dad had certainly grown to love me and treat me as one of his own daughters. It was wonderful to feel so blessed. However, there was still something missing. We did not have a home to call our own. That afternoon, as I drove toward the farmhouse we were still renting, I was daydreaming. Thinking about all the positive changes that had taken place, I thanked God for all the blessings He had given my family and me. As I drove along, I felt myself being nudged to look to my left, and there in a yard I noticed a "For Sale" sign. I could not understand what it was God wanted me to see.

As I continued driving, I started thinking about what was going on around me. I had been detoured from my normal route because of street repairs. The sun was bright, and the grass had started to grow again, but I could not see anything unusual happening. Then a small voice came to me in a thought: *You and John will buy a house in about three months.* I almost burst into laughter. I certainly could not see any way for us to buy a home when we had no extra money for anything. I could not ignore the very strong impression that had been placed on my mind. I never really understood how I got these premonitions, but somehow, I usually knew when it was from God. I decided it was something I should share with John.

That night after supper, I followed John into the living room to relax. I began telling him about the premonition I had felt on my way home. At first, John's reaction was the same as mine. He started to laugh, then caught himself and said, "Baby, you're probably right. I should know not to question your beliefs or your communication with the Lord."

There were many times when I would try to interpret the thoughts that were given me. More often than not, my interpretations would not make sense, or I would try to figure out ahead of time what God was planning for me. Whenever I did this, I was almost always wrong. John was forever telling me to slow down, to let the Lord show me what He meant in His timing. At times you have to sit back and let

God work in your life. Some of the best works can be done when you are completely trusting in Him for all you do. Then you can look back later and see the beauty in it.

By the end of June, we were given a month to find a place to live because our landlady had promised her brother that he could live in the part of the house that we were presently renting. Frantically, we looked for a place to live. Nothing was working; we could not find a house or apartment that would work for us. Either our children were too old for the lease guidelines or they were too young. We could not win. Sometimes while hunting, we would find a house that was satisfactory, but it was in a bad neighborhood. I was starting to feel very desperate.

John was working about seventy hours a week then and could not help me look for a place. The other condition was that he insisted that Tina and Geoff attend a good school. Finally, we only had a week left to find a place. My district supervisor at the store had just moved and thought that his real estate agent might be able to help. The realtor, Jim, told us about a house in Berea that was for sale. He felt certain that the owner would rent it to us with an option to buy. We made an appointment to meet the real estate agent at that evening.

As John and I pulled into the driveway, we both felt something come over us—a strange sensation. It was a very strong feeling of familiarity, kind of like déjà vu, like we had been there before. Once we followed Jim inside, John and I fell in love with the layout of the house. It was perfect for us. It had everything I wanted my next house to have. It was a ranch-style home with three bedrooms, a big eat-in kitchen, and a fireplace in the living room. It was perfect, including the size. The lot was huge and had a two-car garage in the back. Two beautiful birch trees dressed up the front yard, and three maple trees shaded the entire backyard. John and I knew without a doubt that this house was meant to be ours.

Jim took us to his office so that we could fill out the necessary paperwork. We had to work up some financial data as if we were planning to buy the house. It was necessary for the owner to see that we made enough money to support the payments. In doing so, we qualified to purchase the house, so the seller agreed, knowing that eventually we would be able to obtain a bank mortgage. Jim said that although we could start out with a lease option to buy, it might be a good idea to see if we could get a loan right away.

We tried to explain to him that we did not think our credit ratings would be good enough to work with, but Jim was willing to try anyway. John had the feeling that Jim was being a little pushy with us through the whole ordeal. It seemed that way to me as well. Jim's insistence on doing it his way began to make us a little uncomfortable. Naturally, John decided to confront Jim with what he was feeling. Jim agreed with us. He said he did not understand why he felt the sense of urgency, but it was as if he felt very strongly that he had to get the house for us. In his opinion, he had never experienced this feeling before.

Jim said, "I feel as if this house was meant to belong to you. Does this make any sense to either of you?"

Naturally, John and I agreed, saying that we felt that God was the power behind what was happening. Things moved very quickly, and by the end of that week, we moved into our new house, planning on renting to own. Two weeks later, it was a done deal—signed, sealed, and delivered—but not the way we thought. After renting for two weeks, our paperwork was swiftly expedited and we bought our lovely ranch home. We closed on the house and the deed was in our names.

Praise God! I have been told that it takes three to six months to obtain approval for a Federal Housing Administration loan. It is a tedious, long, and drawn-out process. Jim was right, though—the house was meant to be ours. Everything went so fast, and everyone involved pushed the paperwork as if they were up against some kind of invisible deadline. For us to have it done in one month was truly a miracle.

Chapter 18

$\mathcal{T}$he next day at work, I pulled out a Scripture from my favorite glass box, and this is what it said:

> In this you greatly rejoice, though now for a little while you may have had to suffer grief in all kinds of trials. These have come so that your faith—of greater worth than gold, which perishes even though refined by fire—may be proved genuine and may result in praise, glory, and honor when Jesus Christ is revealed. (1 Peter 1:6–7 NIV)

For me to understand this Scripture on my own is impossible. What did it have to do with our lives? I guess we would come to find out.

By September, we were fairly well situated in our new home. Tina and Geoff were back in school. It felt good to come home from work to our new house every day. I could not thank God enough for what He had done for us. When I think about the Scripture, I realize that we were tested, yet believed that God could work a miracle for us, and He did. He gave use our house when it was an impossible situation. But when you trust God in all things, He provides. Although you may go through more than you think you can handle, the Lord blesses you for not giving up.

You would think by now that our future looked bright and hopeful. It seemed that way, too. Like I said before, though, sometimes when things are going well, we hit a snag. Today, when I look back at this "snag," I think the word is an understatement. We were all so busy getting used to our house that no one seemed to realize that John was having difficulty. He was beginning to feel tired more often than usual. In the past, it always seemed like he had enough energy for two men. Now he was frequently tired.

Plus, he had been noticing that his skin was bruising easily. Since he had been working so many hours, we thought maybe he was just overworked.

I finally talked John into seeing a doctor. John went to see Dr. Waghray and afterward called me from the doctor's office to tell me that he would be late. It seemed that Dr. Waghray felt that John should go to the hospital for some tests. When he came home, we talked about this sense of urgency that Dr. Waghray had felt. John said the doctor noted a rapid weight loss along with the bruising, which might be indicative of a chance of leukemia. What did he mean by this? What was leukemia exactly? According to John, leukemia was a blood disorder. Trying very hard to calm me down, John insisted we not worry until the test results were back.

I had not met Dr. Waghray yet, but I thought that he must be a very good doctor to detect this condition so quickly in John. If it were true that John was sick, I was glad that we had found out and could do something about it. According to John, Dr. Waghray was pleasant to talk to and probably of Indian descent. I figured he must be pleasant to speak to if he convinced John to go to the hospital. John hated hospitals, but he liked Dr. Waghray immediately. I knew this was a good thing under the circumstances.

Three days after John had gone to see him, Dr. Waghray called. He left a message for John to call him as soon as possible. That evening, John placed a call to the doctor's office and found out that the test results had come back positive. There were signs of leukemia. Dr. Waghray insisted that John see a cancer specialist. By recommendation, John went to see Dr. Jon Reisman. This whole new problem in our lives made us both very nervous. No matter what, we still had hoped that it was all a big mistake. Dr. Reisman also found signs of the cancer in John's blood tests.

For more proof, John went to St. John West Shore Hospital for a bone marrow scan. This was a test that was to be done as an outpatient. John went to the hospital, stayed in a regular room for the day, and was prepared for the test. None of this medical testing made me feel comfortable—especially knowing that his was the same hospital that I had gone to after John had hurt me. Was it a bad omen? I hoped not. Chills went up my spine as we made our way into the hospital that morning.

When Dr. Reisman came in to set up the test for John, I had to leave the room. Before I left, a tall man in his midthirties sat down on the edge of John's bed to explain to both of us what he would be doing. A small incision would be made on John's lower back where marrow is produced in the hip bone. The marrow is located between the joints. A syringe would be used to remove just enough marrow to run some tests. Then, after John was stitched back up, he could rest for about a half an hour before being allowed to return home. They would give him a local anesthetic to numb the area before they began working on him. Once this test was completed, all we could do was wait.

How do you wait for such a thing? A million thoughts went through my mind while waiting on something as devastating as this. It was enough to make me unhinged, detached from reality. The anxiety we felt was draining. What if it really was leukemia, then what? Is it terminal? Could it be treated or cured? We would soon find out.

A week later, we went to Dr. Reisman's office. The doctor came into the waiting room to personally greet us. In his strong accent—which I supposed was German—Dr. Reisman asked us to come into his office. He was very direct. "I'm afraid I have bad news for you. The test results show an advanced case of leukemia." The doctor explained that it was a type of leukemia that usually occurred only in older men. John and I had just turned thirty-seven earlier that year. Dr. Reisman was referring to men in their sixties and older who came down with this disease. The hardest part of the news was that if John had waited one more month, he would have already died. Talk about shocking news!

We were devastated. *This is not really happening*, we thought. Dr. Reisman continued to explain the disease and the different stages one goes through. The words started to fade out as I became consumed in my own thoughts. *Oh, my God. Please help us. This can't be happening. I can't believe John's going to die. No, no, he can't leave me now. Not now. We just got our lives back together. How could You possibly let this happen!* The tears began to surface and it took all the strength I could muster up not to cry. I could not cry—not then. John needed me to be strong for him.

The sound of Dr. Reisman's voice came rushing back. "There are some possible treatments we could use to get you into remission, John, but there are no guarantees they'll work. The first thing we can try is oral chemotherapy. If this does not work, I am afraid we will have to take more drastic measures."

I am not sure how John and I got back to the car; we seemed to be in a daze. The words spoken kept running through my head. John tried to cheer me up by being humorous, making light of it all as if it were not happening to him. For the first time in a very long time, I wanted a drink—not a soft drink. I could consume myself in a bottle of wine. I expressed this to John, knowing quite well that I would be opening up a new problem. John replied with, "Me, too."

He stopped at the next gas station and bought us a grape drink. As he handed it to me with a smile, he said, "We can pretend." The rest of the way home, we were silent.

Chapter 19

$\mathcal{T}$he news of John's illness was very difficult for all of us. Tina and Geoff had grown to love John very much. It had been a gradual growth of affection as all of us tried to understand each other. Nurturing and growing together, we had become a loving family again. It took time to rebuild faith where so many problems had caused downfalls awhile back. The thought of John dying was not a concept that we could believe.

Tina dealt with this news in her own way. Shortly after learning the news, Tina started to run away from home every time John's condition worsened. Tina had lost her grandfather when she was at a very young and impressionable age. The fact that I had divorced her father and taken her far away was another type of loss. She could not stand anymore loss in her life. The only way she could cope with

John's being sick was not to face it. She could not handle losing him, too.

John and I tried our best to show Tina that she was loved and that she should not be afraid of death. Still, until her senior year of high school, Tina continued to take off. Sometimes weeks would go by before she would let us know that she was safe. Having a lot of friends to help us was a blessing. Most of the time when Tina would disappear, people took the time to let me know that they had seen her and she seemed okay. She made it clear each time that she did not want to be found. She would call me once in a while to reassure me that all was well.

It was unnerving for all of us trying to cope with the entire realm of John's illness. My heart ached for Tina and Geoff. John felt the pain of despair and helplessness of not being able to say to all of us that everything would work out okay. No, there was no way of making this nightmare go away. John spent hours talking to the kids about how he felt, how he thought he was letting them down, and that he did not want to die but that we would all meet again someday. John did the very best he could to constantly reassure them that they were loved very much and that much of what he had done in his life was an example of what not to do.

John was always there to hug them when they needed it. He was there to tell them how much they were loved and to stress to them the importance of the "Big R," as he put it: Responsibility. John wanted so much for Tina and Geoff to feel secure in dealing with whatever life threw their way. It was important for them to know that the love he had for them would not go away, that sometimes things do not always turn out the way we want them to. He assured them, as I did, that I loved them deeply and only wanted what was best for them, even when it was necessary to take disciplinary action. We explained that it was done because I wanted to teach them right from wrong.

As time went on, we muddled through as well as we could, struggling to maintain our sanity while we went on doing our daily tasks. Geoff seemed to hold up well under the circumstances. He never understood why Tina would take off when things looked gloomy. Geoff remained calm and quiet as he absorbed everything that went on around him. He found refuge in working on his artwork, diving on the swim team, and running his early morning paper route. Thankfully, there was very little time in his day to think of anything other than getting all of his activities completed. Toward the end, John asked Geoff to be strong for me because I would need to draw from his strength to keep going.

Geoff was very dependable and always there when I needed him during the long, drawn-out, and very intense period of losing John. To this day, I am very proud of the compassion that Geoff showed for John and me. I needed strength from Geoff. I am not so sure that it was right of me to draw it from him, but I could never have coped with the stress of it all without Geoff's help. I never would have made it through this period if Geoff had been the same way as Tina—running off and causing even more worry. Even though I understood why she did it, the loss of her presence caused me much worry.

Tina loved John very much, and John treated her as if she were his own. Geoff was loved also, but there was something very special between John and his little princess. God had blessed us all with the love that John had to share. There was an intense, deep, and dedicated kind of love that we all had for each other. It was a blessing, true and strong. It seemed that there was never a day without a new problem. After graduation from high school, Tina went to Pennsylvania to live with my mother and spend some time with her relatives and old friends. I think, more than anything, that it was becoming harder and harder for her to watch John fade as the leukemia took his strength and his outward appearance became weak and brittle.

Several weeks after Tina had gone to Pennsylvania, we found ourselves without a car that ran. One day as I made my way home on the RTA bus, I could think of nothing but my last conversation with John earlier in the day. I knew he was not doing well, although he tried to convince us that he was okay. I was very concerned about what to expect when I arrived home. I made my way across the plaza parking lot to the field behind it—a shortcut with a path to the street where I lived. As I continued walking faster and thinking about John, I began to have a strong feeling that something was wrong. Once I was close to the house, my heart began to beat faster. I was breathing harder as fear penetrated my mind about what I would find when I opened the door.

The backdoor was unlocked and open. The screen door was the only thing separating me from the events that were about to unfold. I took a deep breath, pulled open the screen door, and yelled in, "Honey, I'm home." There was a moment of silence. Then the sound of slow-moving footsteps came around the door. He was moving slower than I had ever seen him move before. He walked with a cane at that time to help keep his balance. His eyesight had failed to the extent that he could no longer see to drive. John's body had become thin and weak. He was not at all the man I had met so many years ago. Where once there had been a 160-pound man with broad shoulders, now stood a man who seemed only skin and bones. The smiling John that I had known was gone.

I could see from the look on John's face that he was in great pain. He was barely moving. I slowly walked back to the living room with him as he explained that he had taken several Percodan in the last two hours, but nothing had stopped the intensity of the pain he was in. Tears filled his eyes as he explained how his entire body felt like it was ready to explode with pain.

John was scared, and, as in the past, he knew the signs were not good ones. I sat holding his hand, questioning what to do next. He called Dr. Reisman, and he suggested we get John to the hospital immediately. My mind went numb as I tried to think how he would get to the hospital since we had no car. My heart was aching for him, and that old helpless feeling was there—the feeling of not having any control of the situation.

Then the phone rang. My moment of aching was broken up by a new interruption. *Now what?* Reluctantly, I picked up the phone to hear my sister's voice. Always so soft and quiet, her voice seemed hesitant as she explained that there was an accident and that Tina was at the hospital. Inside, I felt like dying. I wanted to scream. I thought, *I can't take any more of this.* I continued to listen as Paula explained that Tina had lacerations on her face and chest. Paula had not wanted to call me until she knew that Tina would be okay. Paula explained more about what had happened.

When Tina entered the emergency room at Mt. Pleasant Hospital, her Aunt Cora was just about to go off duty when she recognized Tina. She stayed with her to assist the doctor. Cora wanted to be sure Tina was all right before she left. Tina's condition made her somewhat helpless. Both her arms were wrapped and her face was patched up as well. She would not be able to take care of herself for at least a few weeks.

My mother and sister assured me that Tina would be all right.

I felt beside myself. There I was sitting with John in our living room as he suffered great pain and had little time left, and I was three and a half hours away from my daughter, who also needed me. I was torn between the two people who were both hurting and needing me. As I explained the situation to John, we both got caught up with Tina's problems for a while and forgot about the reality of John's situation. Both of us were in tears by now. I thanked Paula for calling and told her I would call back after I had heard that Tina was comfortably situated at home with my mother at her house.

The next step was to find someone to take John to the emergency room. Brad, one of John's best friends from work, came over immediately when we called him, and the three of us made our way to the hospital. John, joking as usual and trying to make light of a bad situation, kept us from coming unglued.

As usual, John was right again about his situation. His white blood count was high and his platelets were too low. Dr. Reisman met us there and suggested that John be admitted. However, John did not want to stay, because he felt I needed him more. Dr. Reisman agreed to give John a change of pain medication until the next day and told John he needed to come back in for a platelet transfusion and a high dose of chemotherapy.

John was slightly more comfortable on the way home with the new medication. I was able to call my mom's house and talk with Tina once she was there and resting comfortably. My mind would not rest until I could hear her voice. I was very relieved when I could talk to her. John spoke to her also, assuring her that we loved her and explaining how hard it was for us not to be there with her. This was just one of many situations that seemed to occur as we struggled through each day wondering what tomorrow would bring. Could we cope? How much more could we take? Again, as I started to feel deep despair, a verse came to mind that the Lord would give me in times of trouble.

> He shall cover thee with his feathers, and under his wings shalt thou trust: his trust shall be thy shield and buckler. Thou shalt not be afraid for the terrors

by night; nor for the arrow that flieth by day; nor the pestilence that walketh in darkness; nor the destruction that waste that noonday. (Psalm 91:4–6 KJV)

Dear God, hold us up in these times of deep and lonely emptiness. Help us to know that You are there every moment; that You reach out to us to shelter us from all the world. Help us to know that, no matter what happens, You will get us through. Your arms are stretched out to all of us. We need not worry about any of our needs, for You shall supply them as they are needed. Lord, thank You for being here with us always. Amen.

Chapter 20

*I*t had been nine months since Tina's accident. The days continued to tug at us, creating more walls for us to bang into, and it became more difficult to cope with everything. It was now the beginning of August. The children and John and I had gone through a lot of pain and worry. Geoff went back to school, and I continued to work. John was alone at home in his agony. John was told by his doctor that he only had about a month to live. He went back into the hospital for a new chemotherapy treatment. It put him back in remission once more. How many times had this happened? Dr. Reisman had researched all over the world for different types and combinations of chemotherapy for John to take. It kept him going a lot longer than if he had stopped all treatments earlier. It made him hallucinate and run high fevers, leaving him unable to comprehend what was reality and what was not. He didn't make sense when he tried to talk, but he was still alive.

From the time when we first learned of John's illness until now, a lot had happened with the changes in his medication. At one point, he was put on interferon. The first time he took it, John had started to hallucinate. He became semicomatose, ran a high fever, and had night sweats as well. He almost died the first time he used the drug. It had to be injected, and John was given instructions on how to do this. I was scared. I was trying to cope with all of the side effects that night. In one instance, he saw his mother, although she had been dead since he was a small boy.

We made it through the night, and by the next day, John seemed fine. He told me about his hallucinations and how real they had seemed. There was a long period during which we dealt with the drugs he had to take to stay alive and the side effects they caused. No matter how you looked at it, it was a tough situation. John began to have severe mood swings. One minute he was happy, joking, and having fun; the next, he would be yelling at me, demanding unusual things. Once, he threatened to cut off my head with an ax if I didn't hear him the next time he was talking to me. He would punch holes in the walls, screaming and yelling things that made no sense at all.

John made an appointment with Dr. Reisman so that he would help us understand the behavior that the drug was causing. John explained that when this behavior happened, he knew it was happening but had no control over it. Although he was trying very hard to stop it, he was not able to. It was like being taken over by someone or something. All he knew was that he would rather die than continue to put me and the children through this. Dr. Riesman continued to change John's medication as needed. If the drug usually worked for a six-month duration, John would be lucky to get three months of treatment before it stopped working. It was like clockwork. Every time we were told of something new, we knew exactly how to time it.

Dr. Reisman started looking for options for John far in advance of the expected use of the current drug. He knew that John had analyzed his body's chemistry to a perfect science. The doctor had suggested that John neither smoke nor drink any alcohol because it could kill him. The chemotherapy had destroyed his liver and kidneys. Although John had done very little drinking for a long time, it was the wrong thing to tell him.

After he went home, he tried drinking himself to death. I became fearful because of his past actions. Eventually, I asked him to leave again; I had been through more than I could handle. So long as he would not stop drinking, sick or not, I was not going to be abused again. John was so unpredictable that I never knew what would happen. He was Dr. Jekyll and Mr. Hyde. I never knew whom I would face each day or night.

When Dr. Reisman told John that his liver and kidneys were not functioning well at all, John was not surprised. What the doctor told him gave John a solution—an easy way out. Since John already knew what medications he could and could not handle—which ones made him into a sort of monster—he wanted no part of those. I sought help from our church minister, Doug. He suggested that John and I come to see him regularly. Finally, we got back together and had family counseling and individual counseling for John and me. Doug was wonderful. His understanding and helpful ways brought John to terms with himself. With Doug's help and our faith, we were able to go on. John went from a man who was often violent and left fist holes in the walls to a man who could not get through a day without helping someone else.

Finally, John was too ill to go to church anymore, so he watched it on television. He spent hours on the phone each day talking and sharing what God had done in his life and how his faith had made him a new person. It got to a point where every time someone called to see how he was, John ended up helping them instead. The person he called could not tell from the other end of the calls that he was sick or that he was fading away. Each day, I would come home to hear what new person John had touched with his positive words.

The changes were finally there. John was reading his Bible more. He was sharing what he learned in the Bible with his friends. One of his favorite verses was, "Take my yoke upon you and learn from me, for I am gentle and humble, in heart; and you shall find rest for your soul" (Matthew 11:29 NIV). John felt God was drawing him near and teaching him to lean on Him in all things.

At one time, John would have defended himself in any situation. He would have verbally laid guilt on anyone so that he did not have to accept his own faults. Then a bell went off in his head one day. John realized that he was not nor would he ever be perfect in any way, and that God sent His Son Jesus to die for us because we are sinners. God's love for us has set us free. Until then, John felt he had to be perfect to get into heaven. By reading the Gospel of John and Peter, he learned what he could do to leave his mark behind. John put on the armor of God. He was reading the Bible, and the Scriptures came alive for him. More and more, he read and learned and listened to God's Spirit inside him to guide him through the day. John was finally happy. The Scriptures he referenced transformed his thinking.

> For by grace are ye saved through faith; and that not of yourselves: it is the gift of God: not of works, lest any man should boast. (Ephesians 2:8–9 KJV)

> So then, faith cometh by hearing, and hearing by the word of God. (Romans 10:17 KJV)

When the weather turned to warmth and sun-shine, John sat out in the backyard and listened to a tape by Kataro and talked on the phone. He had a hospital bed in the living room that he would use for naps during the day. At night, he invited his friends over for games of backgammon and chess. People would stay for hours to keep him company. It was good for him, but it often created tensions for me. I knew how tired John was and that he would end up having to sleep long periods of time in between visits from his friends.

John now had a new mission for the rest of his life. He became a farmer. The Bible talks about planting seeds. John was planting seeds everywhere he could. He knew some would fall on deaf ears, but he also knew that some would grow. If only one seed could blossom into something special, then he had done his job. The man I married had not been every-thing he could have been, but God had changed him into a wonderful example of a husband and father.

Why did it have to happen that way? All my life I had wanted someone to love me, love me for who I am. John had loved me to the fullest. In every way, he went beyond any expectations I could ever imagine. Mentally, physically, and spiritually, he had achieved his goals in life. He had made peace with God. Amazingly, in spite of his situation, he was happy. It made me happy to see him that way. He made me feel fulfilled. No matter what, I had lived life to the fullest with him. I had been given someone who loved me and made me feel full again. If God could have come down and held us in His arms, I know it would have been how John made me feel when he held me, because what we had was blessed with God's grace.

It was wonderful to see this change—to feel the change and to experience it with him. Yet I knew that someday I would be alone once more. Would I be ready? Did I have on my breastplate of righteousness?

Finally, my brethren, be strong in the Lord, and in the power of his might. Put on the whole armor of God, that ye may be able to stand against the wiles of the devil. For we wrestle not against flesh and blood, but against principalities against powers, against the rulers of darkness of this world, and against spiri-

tual wickedness in high places.
(Ephesians 6:10–12 KJV)

John was winning his battle—the lifelong struggle to be accepted, to have a family of his own, to have loved ones, to have genuine friends of his own, to have a purpose.

I felt confused. Could this be the end? I thought we were going to build a church. Had I already helped do that through John? Was the church in him? Was it in me? Were we the church?

Chapter 21

$\mathcal{H}$ad we built our inner church? No. How much more would we have to go through? Our finances were gradually getting worse due to John's not being able to work and the fact that John's health insurance policy was not very solid. It did not cover prescriptions for medicine, and we had already spent hundreds and hundreds of dollars each month keeping John alive. John was very concerned about this and how it was affecting our lives. We could lose everything. Our mortgage payments were too far behind, and there was not enough extra money for food and necessities. John talked about the possible loss of our home and how he would do everything possible so this would not happen. He even suggested getting a divorce so that I would not have to be responsible for his debts.

I would not hear of it. If God wanted us together, then we should trust Him for an answer. Since the house was such an important factor, the Lord sent us a sign. Just about the time when we were about to have our house taken away through foreclosure, something happened. A man came knocking at our door one day. Neither John nor I knew him. He introduced himself as the son of the man we bought our house from. It had been over a year since we had bought our house, and we had never talked to the real estate agent since then. We invited him in, and he began to tell us why he was there. Keep in mind that we bought the house in August, and that Jim, the agent, was in a hurry to sell it to us.

This man, Jim's son, brought with him a piece of slate. On it was a wintry scene with words at the top, which said, "Welcome to the Witkowski's." The reason that Jim's son brought the sign to us is because Jim had passed away in November, just three months after we bought the house. Before Jim died, he had this slate painting designed for us. In our hour of despair and grief, we were shocked by this unusual story about a man we hardly knew, who showed he cared for us. He not only helped us obtain our house but had a housewarming gift made for us, somehow perceiving we would still be here and would remain here. John and I felt this was God's way of showing us that He cared and is with us always.

We shared our story with Jim's son, telling him how his father was compelled to sell us our house. We thought it helped Jim's son to know his father had been in touch with the Lord and was probably with Him today. After this incident, John decided I was right: God was by our side. Divorce was not the answer. His new solution was one I did not approve of at all, though. He knew someone who had been on painkillers over a long period of time for physical reasons. Because the pills were habit-forming, his doctor wanted him to get off the drugs, but the patient wanted to continue. John decided to sell half of each prescription he had in order to get enough money to pay for his own medication.

I turned my back on this. I wanted no part of it. The less I knew, the better I felt. Still, I could not blame John for his desire to want to keep us from losing everything. Each time we had a need, whether it was emotional or financial, God continued to help us. He let us know He was there. Even when John became physically depleted, God helped us get through.

I remember waking up one day to find John talking strangely. As he sipped his tea, it was running down his face. He finally realized something was wrong and went to look in the bathroom mirror. When he came out, he was humiliated. His face was twisted to one side. He looked like someone who had had a stroke. "First it was my hair," John said. "Then my legs went bad, then my eyes, and now this." All of the things we normally take for granted, John was losing, one by one. John had suffered a ministroke called Bell's palsy.

This did not stop John, though; he was determined not to let it stand in his way of living as normally as he possibly could. It was so hard to watch the changes take place. I could see the sadness in his eyes as he joked about his condition. Normally, John was good at making people laugh, especially when they didn't feel much like laughing. I wanted so much to help when things like this happened, but I was so helpless. I wanted to make it all go away for him, but all I could do was sit and watch and wait. Just giving John emotional support did not seem enough to me.

I set up a special arrangement with the hospital so John could spend the day with other cancer patients. The program was supposed to help the families who could not be there with their loved ones all of the time. I took John to the home early one morning hoping he would enjoy being with others. The whole thing backfired on me. John was not there more than an hour on the first day when I received a call from the counselor saying John wanted to leave and never return. John said those people were too old and sick; he didn't want to be with sick people.

From this point on, I set up shifts with Pam, Greg, and Sissy (an old friend of John's), along with Elie and myself. We took turns watching him around the clock. John was now at a point where he could no longer comprehend simple things such as knowing what time it was or how or what medication to take. His mind was too far gone. The cancer and radiation he had taken were destroying him mentally. He became childlike, not being able to do much of anything without someone's help. It was heartbreaking. John was a very intelligent person with a photographic memory. Normally, he could recall anything he had learned. All you had to do was ask and he had the answer. As his time on this earth was ending, John still tried to do things he used to do.

One morning, he got up at five thirty wanting to go to McDonald's to buy me breakfast. There was only one problem: he could no longer drive. He looked at me with his puppy dog eyes, like a small child who was being punished, asking if I would drive to McDonald's for him so that he could buy us breakfast. On another occasion, he decided that he wanted to patch one of the holes in the wall of our dining room. He proceeded to get the tools from the garage and bring in a piece of drywall to replace the missing piece. I had to watch him carefully. He could no longer see to hit the nail straight, so he figured he could start the nail through the drywall before hanging it by hammering it on the table. Then he proceeded to nail it to the kitchen table. It was a trial, just trying to control his actions so he didn't destroy the house.

He continued trying to do things like this, most of which took place in the early morning hours when I would have preferred to be sleeping. The one encouraging part of this was that the girls that worked for me at Revelations were always anxious to hear the latest story. This would help me feel some type of release each day. My mental state needed any help it could get.

John continued trying to stay in control. He often had said he would never get so bad that he could not take care of all his bodily functions, nor would he be bedridden. Dr. Reisman said he never saw anything like John's behavior. It was incredible how he never stopped. Most people were completely bedridden much earlier in the progression of the disease. Up until the very end, John never gave up the fight.

Chapter 22

$\mathcal{T}$ he last time John went to his usual weekly appointment at St. John West Shore Hospital for his platelet transfusions, a major change in him was evident. John became less lucid and more anxious. His white blood cell count was dropping again. This became a regular occurrence whenever John's body would go through one of its painful changes. This time was different; he became less lucid and very restless as well.

It was Pam's shift to watch him, so she took him to the hospital that day. When John was there, he said goodbye to all of his favorite nurses. It was as if he knew that he would not see them again. These were times when he was in the hospital more often than he was at home. All of the nurses knew and enjoyed his stays. He brought them candy and ordered pizza for them at lunchtime. He was the perfect patient. Always kind and sympathetic to them and their problems, he would go out of his way to help them out and not be a problem to them.

On the way home from the hospital that afternoon, John and Pam stopped at the park down the street from our house. As they sat there and talked, John told Pam that God had clearly answered his prayers. He now understood the true meaning of real friends and true love. He had always wanted to have true love in his life and a loving wife, children, and true friends. He was happy about his life. John once told me that if he had not met me, he probably would have ended up back in jail to die as an empty and lonely man. He said I had given him the answer to all his prayers, and God was a gracious and loving Father.

That same evening when I came home from work, I was very surprised to find John and Pam in the backyard arguing over him trying to walk to the store. He would not have remembered how to get there, nor could he have walked that far. His frail body could not have carried him that far, but in his mind, he still believed he was strong enough to take the walk. I finally had to call the police to help us get him under control. Once the police talked John into taking his morphine, he started to relax.

Several hours went by, and John never went to sleep. I realized the drug he was taking made him confused at times, but this time it was beyond normal confusion. His sentences were not complete. He thought I was his mother sometimes, his sister Elaine at other times, and, once in a while, he knew it was me, his Nora. About eleven o'clock that night, he finally fell asleep. However, every two hours he would get back up, so it was not a good night for either of us.

In the morning, Sissy came to watch him. While I was at work, some boys had come over to visit Geoff. John was confused and thought they had come to hurt Geoff, so he threatened them, then called the police. Sissy had to explain to the police why John was not making any sense.

That night was even worse than the one before. John slept in even shorter intervals, followed by getting up and doing weird things in the middle of the night. By the time morning came, I was exhausted from following him around to keep him out of trouble. Greg came at about 8:30 a.m. to take over so I could go to work. When I got home that night, John was sitting in the living room trying to take his socks off.

He had given Greg a hard time during the day. Because it was difficult for him to breathe, John decided to take all of his clothes off. In his mind, this made sense. He could no longer communicate with us about what was bothering him. The radiation that he had experienced had done too much damage. The look on Greg's face was heartbreaking. There was so much hopelessness and sadness there as he watched his friend being so helpless and confused. I felt so bad for him, and I told him to go home and get some rest.

From the time Greg left in the early evening until about three o'clock in the morning, John never stopped moving. He would lie down on the hospital bed for about two seconds, then jump up and go to the couch. As soon as his head touched the pillow, he would fall asleep. Then, several seconds later, he would rise up again and make his way to the bedroom. Once he would lie down, he would start all over again. He would be there for a few minutes and jump up and start the circle from the bed to the couch to the hospital bed. Round and round we went. I could not let him do this alone. He was falling too much and hurting himself. His body was beginning to look like it had been beaten up by someone. As I followed him, I kept hoping John would fall asleep so that I, too, could get some rest.

As the hours passed, John stumbled often and was falling more and more. His face was almost all one complete bruise. His back and shoulders as well as his legs were solid masses of purple and black spots. It was horrible. I tried so desperately to help him, yet I was failing miserably. I never felt so helpless in all my life. I was so tired. I found myself screaming out loud, "God, please, why do You let him go on this way? He is killing himself. Please help him. Take him home. Don't let this go on anymore. Please, Lord." I was in tears. I had no energy left, and I was hysterical and losing control.

In the early morning hours, I called for an ambulance. However, they warned me ahead of time that if John would refuse to go with them, they could not take him. I knew that would happen, so I told them not to come. What else was there for me to do? Then I called my doctor and he said to find a way to get him to the hospital. When I called the attending emergency room doctor, he listened to my situation and said he would stay on duty until I brought John. By 6:00 a.m., I called my neighbors. Pam and Bob agreed to come over and help me get John to the hospital. John helped us dress him willingly because we told him he would be going for a ride. We put him in the backseat of our car so that Bob could watch over John as we made our way to the hospital.

Once we got there, a policeman brought us a wheelchair. As we tried to get him out of the backseat, John jumped into the front seat where he sat clapping his hands saying, "Let's go. Let's go." He thought he was just then starting out on a ride. He had no idea where he was or how he got there.

We finally wheeled John into the emergency room, where the doctor who was waiting for us took over. They took John into one of the emergency rooms and hooked him up to a heart monitor. They quickly found out that he was in cardiac arrest. John continued to fight for his every last breath and his dignity. He pulled the monitor off and tried to get out of bed. It was the same thing, only now I understood why it was so important for John to fight so hard. Lying flat made it impossible for him to breathe.

The doctor explained to me that John could not breathe and that his heart had been failing. Most likely, it had started three days earlier when he had received his platelet transfusion. He was behaving strangely because the platelet transfusion had put him into congestive heart failure. With his heart not pumping properly, the oxygen to his brain was insufficient and he could not think clearly. In order to control the situation, the doctor had to have John restrained and heavily medicated, which allowed John to relax more easily.

Chapter 23

One hour had passed and John was now in arm restraints, still struggling to get out of bed. A young police officer took an interest in our situation. He, too, was supposed to be off duty, but like the doctor, was still there trying so hard to help John. By this time, John had been given a large dose of Haldol. This was a type of drug used to calm down patients who were out of control. Even after this, John continued to struggle. Finally, the doctor came in and gave him another shot. As they monitored him, John finally stopped struggling. The police officer no longer had to help me hold him down, yet he stayed until John was admitted, and we were safely set up in a hospital room.

The support that we were given both in the emergency room as well as on the floor was incredible. Everyone had such big hearts. I was so thankful for all of their help and understanding. Finally, John started to drift off into a deep sleep. I finally saw him resting peacefully. This was the first time in four days that either of us was even a little relaxed. Praise be to God. John drifted deeper and deeper into sleep until the doctor said he was in a coma and was unaware of anything going on around him. He was no longer in pain, and I think this was the most reassuring news I heard. There was a small bit of comfort deep inside me knowing that John was not suffering anymore and that all those months of excruciating pain had ended.

As he lay there asleep, unable to communicate, somehow I knew he could hear me. I continued to talk to John, letting him know how much he was loved. I told him that if someone—perhaps his mother or another family member—came for him to take him to the house of the Lord, that it was okay for him to go. Somehow, I knew John would not die on Thanksgiving Day. For John and the rest of his family, holidays were always days that they wished never existed. They had many bad memories of holidays as children, and they all had a tendency to pretend there were no such days on the calendar. Once John and I were together, that all changed. He showed me how important it is to create new memories where bad ones existed. John grew to love holidays. We learned to make them happy and exciting. That was why I felt in my heart that John would hang on until the day had passed.

While John learned to live and love, I learned from him. One Fourth of July, John took us to see the fireworks at Edge Water Park in Lakewood, Ohio. He wanted me to have a brand-new memory of this holiday, a day that had become hard for me to handle since the death of my father. My father had been buried on the Fourth of July, and for Dad, that was good. He had fought in three wars and had been in the service for over twenty years. He was very patriotic, and I think this was in the grand plan when he chose his final day on earth. From the stories I had told John about my father, John had learned to admire him. Most of all, John used to say, "Your father had a great deal of courage, for without it, he could not have had the strength to take his own life."

There were many days when John would be in so much pain that he wished he had the courage to do what my father had done. Yet he knew that it was something I could not have handled at all. John promised that he would never kill himself, no matter what. Sometimes I wished he had not made that promise since it was so difficult to watch him suffer so much.

There is a message in that Fourth of July story. Although John hated crowds and confusion and too much noise, he pushed that hatred of holidays and crowds out of his mind so he could do something for us. He wanted us to see the fireworks because it was something he knew we would enjoy very much. The day was fantastic. The swimming, the picnic lunch, and the evening fireworks were all fabulous. After that special Fourth of July, I learned to enjoy what the present had in store rather than remember the pain of the past.

The day was long, and the night was even longer. During this time, friends and family came to see him for what would be their last time. Goodbyes were necessary for some, but for others, they could not bear to see how he looked. He probably did not weigh more than eighty-five pounds and seemed almost a skeleton. The strong man with the long blond-brown hair was now gone. Who would have ever known that his life would end with so much suffering? As I sat on the edge of his bed and held his hand, I could still feel a sense of consciousness about John.

It was ironic that John didn't pass on until the next day. It had been exactly two years to the day since John had beaten me so badly. I felt that John knew. It was almost as if it was his way of saying he was sorry. By leaving the world on a day that was full of bad memories for me, I believe he was trying to tell me that our lives together had replaced the bad things that had happened. We had replaced the pain with love and sharing.

There was a kind of happy thought going through my mind that John was not going to spoil a holiday. Even his dying on the twenty-third, the next day, would not be a happy memory, but it was his way of saying goodbye and of saying, "I love you." It was his way of telling me, in the only way he had left, that his life had been lived with meaning and purpose. He had gone from feeling like nothing to being someone, a person who could and did make a difference in this life.

What had John learned? It wasn't immediately clear. The dream of the crumbling church—it was John. Yet John was not dead. The white powder that I carried out of the church after his memorial service was God's Spirit inside John's soul. The most important part of him would live on. We would have his memories. All the things he did and the happiness he created—all were amazing moments in time. Although there was the good and the bad, the good always outweighed the bad with John.

He had sowed his seeds in all of us. He did his farming well. His physical death would be just that—physical. John not only lives on in the hearts of all who knew him but his spiritual self was saved. His existence in heaven will last for eternity. The power of God's Spirit was saved in a brokenhearted man—a man who learned to accept who he was and where he was in his life with his family, friends, and, most of all, his God.

Before John passed over to the other side, he found his own way of saying goodbye to me. Sitting at his side, I watched as his eyes began to search around the room. Was he looking for me? Or was he looking beyond the hospital room, beyond the natural realm that we exist in? I made my way to the other side of the bed where John looked my way.

"I am here, John. I am with you," I said. "If someone is here for you, it is okay for you to go. I love you, but it is time. Go, John. It's okay. It's okay. We will meet again. Goodbye, my baby, goodbye."

At that moment, John rose up in bed, breathed his last breath, and drifted off to a place where he could have eternal peace without any kind of pain or heartache.

Chapter 24

*W*ould John's death be the end of a complete life for me? Would I feel alone forever? Was that the last chance for a fulfilled life? Would the rest of my life be lonely and uneventful? It felt that way for a long time. I pondered forever over the question of what led us to each other. Was John the church? Was I? Was God's plan complete?

No, it was not complete, and it may never be. You see, God works in our lives every day, every moment. His plan goes on and on. I do not believe things that happen are coincidental. I believe that we choose the direction we go in, but there is a higher power that moves around us, helping us as we go. This is a dimension beyond the natural realm in which we live. The angels that walk the earth, both good ones and bad alike, are in that dimension. The Holy Spirit also ministers to us, guiding us as we go. Although we have a higher source to help us, we will always make mistakes. My life with John had many problems, yet the truth is that we make mistakes along the way that are damaging to our straight path and a better future. We still have to keep going, believing in God's grace and forgiveness.

We were both inexperienced Christians. We did not know all that the Scriptures taught, but we learned along the way. I still ask myself why our lives worked out the way they did. I may never know all the right reasons about the twists and turns we took. But I do know this: God is a loving God, one who loves unconditionally. John and I shared the same kind of love—unconditional love. Yet, God loves us so much more than we could ever begin to understand. This is why He sent His Son to die for us—so that we could have eternal life.

If you do not have a personal relationship with Jesus, I suggest you ask Him into your life. Life is not worth living without God. Jesus is the best friend you could ever want and, most importantly, He will never leave you. The love God had for John was what kept him going. The changes he made are there to see. As the days and years went by, John learned to accept his own faults, to work at making the necessary changes in his life, to be happy with the life he had, and to return the love that we all had for him.

John's favorite Scripture was, "For by grace are ye saved through faith; and that not of yourselves: it is the gift of God: not of works, lest any man should boast" (Ephesians 2:8–9 KJV). Once John realized that none of us would ever be perfect or sin-free, a bell went off inside his head. He finally knew that he was only human, and to err is only human, that he would never be perfect, and that God would meet him right where he was in his life. John knew from that day forward that he would no longer have to strive for perfection in order to ask God to help him in his life.

To this day, some of our friends still question why I stayed with John when there had been so many times that doing so was difficult. God's powerful love never seemed to run out. He taught both of us about true forgiveness. Love is a choice we make. We can choose to forgive and continue to love, or we can choose not to forgive. I had made so many mistakes in my life that I did not want to stop trying. What we had for each other was unconditional love. When you love someone unconditionally, you are able to forgive. You accept that individual for whom he or she is, not what you expect of him or her. If we could better understand the love that God has for us, it would be so much easier for us to live our lives to the fullest. It is so simple, yet complex. We can only give what we have to give. We can only share what is inside of us if we are willing to do so.

Jesus was a perfect example of everything for which God stands. Why do we make it more difficult than it is? Human nature, I suppose. We have the freedom to choose—the ability to trust God in the direction of our lives or to make our own judgments. You could say it was all a farce, or that I imagined it, or that maybe I am crazy. I don't think so. You see, on the day of my intimate encounter with the Lord, He told me I would write a book someday. And I did. Furthermore, if you have just read it, then the church is still growing. His Word is reaching people every-where, trying to bring hope to a struggling world. It is not too late for us if we start to make changes.

Again, I asked, could John's death be the end, the middle, or just the beginning? Did I grieve for John? I felt sorrow and pain for a long time, and although I had the support of family and friends, it was not enough. One night, I had a dream that changed my vision and direction for all things in my life. I was standing on one side of a four-lane highway. I could see straight ahead where the sun was about to rise. Heavy traffic passed by in both directions, and the sound of wheels zipped past in a hurried, blurry motion. I continued to look beyond the highway to the other side of the freeway. Against the sun, I saw the shadow of a man. He stood motionless, watching me from the other side. As the sun began to rise and the light became visible, I could see it was John. He waved tome as he smiled so happily and then motioned for me to come across to him. As the pace of the traffic slowed, I started to cross over. I stepped onto the pavement, and my legs became very heavy, and I could not move. I felt helpless.

When John realized my condition, he moved across to get me. I could tell there was no hesitation in his thinking whether it was okay to do this or not. He appeared to be taking a chance and scooped me into his arms, ran back to his side, and gently stood me on my feet. As my feet touched the ground, I began to feel as good as new again. The feeling of total joy and peace came over me. I could feel John was very happy. Perfect peace and beauty were everywhere. John told me he had something he wanted to show me, so we walked to a mansion in the distance, talking and laughing as we went. He looked wonderful. He was happy, healthy, and there was a glow about the color of his skin. If this was heaven or anything like it, there was nothing to fear.

Once we made our way into this huge building, I could see the lobby was circular and enormously widespread. The ceiling was more than three stories high. Each floor had a balcony that allowed you to see the entire entrance and foyer. It was absolutely magnificent. The chandelier that hung from the middle of this area was breathtaking with all the glimmer and sparkle of the styles of the 1800s. When we reached the second floor, John told me that he had been preparing a place for us. He said it was our mansion and that all of our family would live there. As we stood looking over the first-floor balcony, I could see that the bottom floor was full of stores, one of every kind that I had told John I wanted to open. The dream and everything about it was as warm and wonderful as the day of my close encounter with the Lord.

We made our way to the freight elevator in the back of the second floor. As we did, we talked and laughed, having such a good time. John told me he wanted to show me something else he was working on. The elevator opened, and I could see bolts of carpeting that John was going to lay on the third floor. He wanted me to go up to the third floor with him and pick out some color schemes for the rooms. We walked and talked for a while, and I understood that he could not be with me because he had so much to do. Heaven was a wonderful place. He was not alone and he was definitely happy.

Then, somehow, I knew I had to leave. There was no time left; I had to hurry. John ran back with me to the highway, but as he kissed me goodbye, I knew that when my life was over, we would meet again someday. I crossed over the highway, and this time the sun was setting behind me. The feelings I had of fear and heartache that had consumed me before I crossed over the first time had disappeared. When I awoke, I felt the love and peace I had known so many years ago when I first felt God's presence.

From that day forward, I began to heal—mind, body, and soul. There are many roads and paths to choose from as we travel through life. We are easily distracted along the way, causing us to be discouraged. Do not let this get in your way. Believe in new beginnings, new hopes, and peace and joy for bright tomorrows.

Nothing is impossible for God.

Therefore, the redeemed of the Lord shall return, and come with singing unto Zion; and everlasting joy shall be upon their head: they shall obtain gladness and joy; and sorrow and mourning shall flee away. (Isaiah 51:11 NIV)

Epilogue

*I*t seems like forever since those days of so much destruction, pain and sorrow. My life has changed in numerous ways. I have traveled a continuous journey seeking the Lord in all that I do. Do not ever think that your life will be perfect, because it won't be. It's not possible in this life. But there is such comfort in knowing that God's love and compassion surpasses all comprehension of the world we live in. I am so looking forward to eternity where we won't have to feel pain, sorrow, or any kind of unhappiness.

Over the years, God has given me a new life. He has graced me with my husband, Dennis, who encouraged me to write this book. Dennis has been supportive in all my endeavors over the years. He is everything I needed and never had in a marriage in the past. Without his love and patience with me through the writing of this book, I could never have completed this project. While I worked on the book, Dennis worked on a project of his own: he built us a beautiful new home that we moved into just before Christmas in 2003.

My children, Tina and Geoff, have forgiven the mistakes I made in my life that affected theirs, and they are now both happily married. I am very proud of them as well as humbled by the way God has healed their hearts and given them success and happiness.

Our family has grown. Dennis has two sons, Todd and Kevin, who are very much a part of our family and a wonderful addition to our lives. We are proud of all our children and their families, including the seven grandchildren with whom we have been blessed.

I can recall another impression that the Lord had given me when I had my day with Him on the way to Johnstown so many years ago. He said I would have two more sons. I never understood that statement. A few years ago, when I reviewed the things that God had spoken to me, I realized the sons He spoke of were Todd and Kevin.

The past created a new avenue that allowed me to be a mentor for other women. This happened as result of my own suffering I had gone through in the past. I have such a passion to help women who are hurting emotionally. My heart's desire to help women continues to grow. In the past, my retail and management background gave me plenty of opportunities to mentor women. My career took a turn when I went to work for one of the largest communications companies in the United States in the marketing and sales division, where I became extremely successful, but that wasn't enough. I decided that I wanted to be able to teach and train women how to transform their lives positively through biblical teaching while they learn how to heal from sins of their past. I have been teaching and training women biblically now for many years. To this day, I teach women biblical principles for life based on God's Word. There is no better teacher than God himself!

I believe God has given me all of these wonderful opportunities because I trust in Him with my life. There is no greater comfort than the peace that surpasses all understanding when God is in the driver's seat. I wouldn't want to trust my own abilities to do anything if the Lord wasn't in control. For He knows the plans He has for you, plans to prosper you, not to harm you. His plans will give you hope for a better future (Jeremiah 29:11, paraphrased). Please keep in mind that His plans for you also include equipping you to achieve the goals at hand. These things are His promises for you. Don't be afraid to follow Him. He knows your past as well as your future. He loves you and wants a relationship with you.

Reach out to Him now. He is waiting for you. You will never regret that you did. God bless you in all things, and may the love of Jesus guide you. He is the greatest friend you will ever have. He will never leave you or forsake you.

About the Author

*N*ora White is a speaker for Stonecroft Ministries. Previously she worked for Salem Communications in Cleveland, Ohio at *95.5 The Fish Radio Station*. Nora had her own radio show called *Hearts for Heaven* on WHKW 1220 AM, which is now podcasted. Her passion is art, and as a Creative Art Therapy Specialist, she encourages those who are disabled by expanding their abilities to be creative in ways that they can express themselves through art. She is also a ministry leader who teaches women Biblical truth for life.

CPSIA information can be obtained
at www.ICGtesting.com
Printed in the USA
BVHW070559240221
600901BV00007B/513

9 781644 689318